YouTube
WORLD
RECORDS

DON'T TRY THIS AT HOME

Some of this book's clips feature stunts performed either by professionals or under the supervision of professionals. Accordingly the publishers must insist that no one attempt to re-create or re-enact any stunt or activity performed on the featured videos.

Published in 2022 by Welbeck
An Imprint of Welbeck Non-Fiction Limited,
part of Welbeck Publishing Group.
Based in London and Sydney.
www.welbeckpublishing.com

Design and layout © Welbeck Non-Fiction Limited 2022
Text © Welbeck Non-Fiction Limited 2022

A CIP catalogue record for this book is available from the British Library.

ISBN 978 1 80279 204 1

Editor: Ross Hamilton
Design: Eliana Holder & Tall Tree
Production: Rachel Burgess

Printed in Dubai

10 9 8 7 6 5 4 3 2 1

YouTube

WORLD RECORDS

ADRIAN BESLEY

WELBECK

CONTENTS

INTRODUCTION

Welcome to the only records book that enables you to see the records being broken for yourself. Enter the short URL or scan the QR code into your phone, tablet, laptop or computer and witness history being made across the world.

The fastest, biggest, highest, thinnest – all over the world people are united by a fascination with extraordinary achievements. We all love a record-breaker. Whether it is a hundredth of a second being shaved off a famous sporting record or the first recording of a fantastically bizarre new category, we share a love of discovering who and what. Till now, the only thing missing has been our chance to actually see the record-breakers in action…

That's where YouTube comes in. This global resource is open to anyone to upload their videos. It contains literally thousands of record-breaking clips, from the most well-known to the completely obscure. Some have millions of views, while others remain virtually undiscovered.

Among the gems available to view are the tallest bonfire in the world; the longest time spent by a human in virtual reality; the fastest speed reached by a human in an Iron Man-esque jet suit; the fastest robot fish in the world; landing on Mars; and a giant kitten the size of a large dog!

This book is your guide to the best of the record-breaking videos on YouTube. It leads you to the most exciting, the most thrilling, the most interesting and the most ridiculous videos on the site. Just read through the brief description and then use the short URL address or the QR code to access the clip – all, of course, completely for free.

HIGH-FLYING RECORDS

Don't look down! It's time to meet some of the sky-high heroes of the record-breaking world. These are some vertigo-immune daredevils who don't know the meaning of fear.

The Wing King

http://y2u.be/eHPZPNzJwLA

On a hot day in May 2017, Fraser Corsan jumped from a plane, 35,508 feet (10,823 metres) above the Californian desert. It's minus 137 degrees Celsius and all he's wearing is a wingsuit, but Fraser is a man on a mission. He was aiming to break a handful of records, but atmospheric conditions have limited him to one: pure speed. On exiting the plane, Fraser immediately hit a speed of 249 mph 400 km/h). He was going so fast that he saw cars going backwards on a motorway, 5 miles (8 km) directly below him – fast enough to make him the world's fastest unassisted human.

WORLD'S FASTEST HUMAN

MOST ROPE JUMPERS TOGETHER

◄ 1,2,3… Jump

http://y2u.be/6SvExJadB78

When your mum says, "And if all your friends jumped off a bridge, would you do it too?" show her this clip. There are 245 of them, many of them probably friends, on a bridge in Hortolandia, near Sao Paulo, Brazil. On the signal, they all jump together from the 98-foot (30-metre) high bridge. Oh, and they're bound together and suspended from the bridge with rope. These thrill-seekers are not bungee jumpers but rope jumpers – their supporting lines having no elasticity – and never before have so many leapt into the unknown en masse.

Basket Case

https://youtu.be/evMG2atXH2c

Basketball legend and Harlem Globetrotter Hammer Harrison stands 6 foot, 9 inches (2.6 metres) tall, so he already nets from quite a height, but here he ascends to 13,000 feet (4 kilometres) in a light aircraft, skydives and attempts a slam dunk. This might be the stuff hoop dreams are made of, but when he's in freefall he's travelling at 120 mph (193 km/h)? Surely, he's mad to attempt such a feat? After all, he's only got one shot at it – and he hasn't even got a helmet on.

▶ Over the Edge

http://y2u.be/h-Z8_qsQYXc

Imagine taking a leap from, say, the top of the Leaning Tower of Pisa, past jagged rocks and into a small pool beneath. In August 2015, in a world-record cliff-jump attempt, Brazilian-born daredevil Laso Schaller plunged almost 200 feet (60 metres) from a ledge into Switzerland's famed Cascata del Salto waterfall. Six oxygen tents were aerating the water in order to give him a softer landing, but Schaller hit the water outside of his intended landing zone – at a speed of around 76 mph (123 km/h). This high-quality video shows the death-defying jump from every angle, including the view from a camera mounted to his helmet.

HIGHS AND LOWS

These record-breakers have gone to extreme heights (or as low as they can go) in order to get their names in the record-books.

▼ New Heights

https://youtu.be/ySzYnwJ6JqU

To mark 872 years since the founding of Moscow, these tightrope walkers have taken celebrations to new heights. Those on the ground can only stand, stare and hold their breath as a group of international tightrope walkers attempt to cross a wire stretched between two of the city's tallest skyscrapers. The wire is over 800 feet (245 metres) long and at a height of 1,150 feet (350 metres). It's clearly quite windy up there and the sky-walkers don't appear to be wearing harnesses, so it's incredibly tense, particularly when one of the them casually stops in mid-air to spread some love!

1,150-FOOT (350M) HIGH TIGHTROPE

Breathtaking!

http://y2u.be/YtryV9qItsg

Next time you're at your local swimming pool, see how long you can hold your breath underwater. Can you do 30 seconds? Or maybe 45, if you really fill your lungs? This exercise will give you some appreciation of Canadian William Winram's 2013 record dive into the Dead Sea at Sharm el-Sheikh in Egypt. Will took a single breath and held it for 3 minutes and 8 seconds, using a sled to help him descend 475 feet (145 metres) – for comparison, New York's Statue of Liberty is just 300 feet (92 metres) high – and a rope and monofin to speed his return to the surface.

◀ Hot Wire

https://youtu.be/KkNiJgbL05Q

Slackline walking demands intense concentration and incredible balance – but it's even harder when a volcano is spitting out red-hot rocks all around you. Alexander Schulz and Rafael Bridi set a new record by being the first to walk a slackline over an active volcano when they crossed the Yasur crater on Tanna Island in the Pacific Ocean on an 853-foot (260 metre)-long tightrope. As well as the sizzling rocks being fired at them, they also had to contend with suffocating sulphuric ash, which was almost hot enough to melt the line, and strong winds that threatened to toss them into the bubbling lava shooting from the volcano.

WORLD RECORD FOR HIGHEST FREE SLACKLINING

Split Seconds

https://youtu.be/UHEyvVgRd7U

Anyone new to roller-skating knows that feeling when your feet head in different directions and you throw yourself to the ground before your body splices in two. Well, Indian teenager Shristi Dharmendra Sharma embraces that feeling. She was an ice-skating limbo world record holder at 13 years old, and four years later she took the roller-skating record too. With her body at a seemingly impossible angle, she did the splits while roller-skating at speed under bars just inches from the ground, sliding under a series of 10 bars in a mere 1.69 seconds.

A Fine Line

https://youtu.be/nLCdMmhWqaM

Lapporten, a U-shaped valley in Lapland in northern Sweden, is one of the most iconic landscapes in this beautiful mountain region. It is here that four German tightrope walkers set out to cross the world's longest ever highline. Breath-taking in terms of both scenery and bravery, the project saw a line set 1969 feet (600 metres) high, spanning 7054 feet (2150 metres) between two Arctic mountain peaks. The four walkers were at the mercy of the winds that sweep through the snow-capped valley, but lead by Quirin Herterich, who trod the wire barefoot, they set a new record that will take some beating.

CHAMPION LIMBO ROLLER SKATER

YOUTUBE HITS RECORDS

In just over 10 years, YouTube has grown to be a part of the daily lives of millions of people. No surprise, then, that it now has its own illustrious record-holders.

▶ Single Out

https://youtu.be/awkkyBH2zEo

They may not be as well-known as their fellow K-pop band BTS, but the South Korean girl group Blackpink have their own dedicated global following. Their fans are called Blinks and they ensure that the group chart in every continent and that the individual members are just as successful in their solo endeavours. In 2021, Lisa became the third of the group's four members to release solo material. Within 24 hours of the music video for her first single, 'LaLisa', being posted online it had received 73.6 million views – nearly 10 million more than previous record holder, Taylor Swift.

YOUTUBE'S MOST WATCHED VIDEO

◀ Shark Attack

https://youtu.be/XqZsoesa55w

On 2 November 2020, four years after it was uploaded, an American campfire children's song, remixed by a Seoul-based company and featuring a nine-year-old New Zealander of Korean–Scottish descent, became the most-viewed YouTube video of all time, surpassing Luis Fonsi's "Despacito" with 7.04 billion views. "Baby Shark", as infuriating as it is endearing, has so far become World Series winners Washington Nationals' theme song, been launched as a breakfast cereal, and has even been performed by anti-government protesters in the Lebanon. Altogether now… "Baby Shark, doo doo doo doo doo dooo…"

No Ordinary Joe

https://youtu.be/6v-a_dpwhro

PE With Joe on YouTube was one of the positive stories of 2020 in the UK. Already a popular online personality, self-styled "body coach" Joe Wicks introduced daily 30-minute workouts when the UK went into lockdown. Aimed at keeping children fit, they were an immediate success, not only with kids but with their families, too. They raised over half a million pounds for charity and earned Joe an MBE, as well as a place in the record books. On 24 March 2020, towards the end of his first week, this video received 55,185 live viewers – a new record for most viewers for a fitness workout live stream on YouTube.

Cause for Concern

https://youtu.be/ISxSLCdmBXY

It was billed as the "never-ending video" and it could have been just that: a record that could never be broken. When the band Twenty One Pilots released their single "Level of Concern", the band invited fans to submit videos to form a constant live stream that changed every time the song restarted. "Dance, animate, dress up, get creative, be weird and have fun," they said, and the fans did just that – for 178 days. When they finally "accidentally" pulled the plug six months after release it was officially the longest music video of all time.

▲ Up, Up and Away

https://youtu.be/R6WyUlvHKAE

MOST-VIEWED LIVE STREAM

The classic short movie, *The Red Balloon*, ends with a boy flying over Paris as he hangs on to a fistful of balloons. This was the inspiration for Illusionist and performer David Blaine's 2020 stunt, which set a new YouTube record for live viewings. Blaine has said he trained for the event for two years, getting a pro sky diver rating and a pilot's licence before the real planning even began. Nevertheless, it's a potentially perilous caper as he ascends nearly 25,000 feet (7620 metres) above the spectacular Arizona desert while hanging from a cluster of balloons.

SPEED AND ACCURACY

Another selection of quick-on-the-draw records. Here accuracy is just as important as speed: one false move could mean death, a dodgy haircut or a customer questioning their receipt.

▶ A Long Shot

https://youtu.be/trW9rxpSBxA

The Australian YouTube team, How Ridiculous, have made an art of breaking records – especially the highest basketball shot, which they have repeatedly broken. Their latest attempt took place at the spectacular Maletsunyane Falls in Lesotho, Africa, where the huge gorge provided the perfect drop zone. Watch as the ball sails through the air for an astounding 660 feet (201 metres) before dropping through the net without touching the sides. It looks easy, but the three Aussies spent eight hours a day for six days attempting the world record shot. They estimated they had attempted around 800 shots without success.

▶ Join the Club

http://y2u.be/6MGlIE2UIII

Yeah, juggling – I know. It's definitely the most boring of circus skills, but put your prejudice aside and watch this guy in action because it's pretty amazing. In September 2016, before busy rail commuters at Toronto's Union Station, Cirque du Soleil's Rudolf Janecek became the fastest five-club juggler in the world. In a whirl of silver clubs and lightning hands, Rudolph shuffles along as he completes 429 rotations in over 30 seconds. In fact, Rudolf threw and caught the clubs so fast that the adjudicators had to review the video in slow-motion before awarding him the record.

FASTEST CLUB JUGGLER

▶ Put Your Feet Up

https://youtu.be/EOFxgwzADjU

For those bikers who don't get enough of an adrenaline hit from just going superfast, pulling a "highchair wheelie" at the same time definitely takes things to another level. A highchair involves sitting on the bike's fuel tank with both legs hanging over the handlebars. Some say it's dangerous, others say it's mad, but British stunt rider Jonny Davies says bring it on! He pops a massive highchair while going at an astonishing 109 mph (176 km/h) to set a new speed record for the stunt.

▼ Crack the Whip

http://y2u.be/C9FsGHM6AaY

THE FASTEST WHIPPER IN THE WORLD

Indiana Jones eat your heart out. Nathan 'Whippy' Griggs is the whip king of the world and has the records to prove it. He holds the fastest records with both one and two hands, and possesses the longest whip in the world at over 329 feet, 7.5 inches (100 metres) long (you can see that on YouTube too – check the sidebar). Wielding 6-foot, 7-inch (2-metre) whips made of kangaroo leather, Nathan demonstrates stamina, skill and incredible co-ordination as he amasses 614 cracks in a minute using two whips. And, in case you're interested, that crack you hear is the whip breaking the sound barrier – over 750 mph (1,200 km/h).

Mr Big Shot

https://youtu.be/YNqyp8t3w68

This world record is not only an impressive display of skill and expertise from golfer Marcus 'The Bullet' Armitage and racing driver Paul O'Neill, but it's also maximum fun to watch. As they try to set a record for the farthest golf shot hit into a moving car, their banter and reactions to their near misses are beautifully captured – none more so than Armitage's shirt-removing celebration for a shot that is quickly judged to be too short. When they finally set a new world record of 909 feet (277 metres), you can't help but feel pleased for both of them.

15

THE NEED FOR SPEED!

Whoosh! There's no substitute for pure lightning strike speed and these guys have all taken the needle into the red with power, guts and a little madness ...

▶ Lightning Bolt

http://y2u.be/4gUW1JikaxQ

"I am trying to be one of the greatest, to be among Ali and Pelé," said Usain Bolt, prior to competing in his final Olympics. That he was going to succeed was never in doubt. Usain Bolt is the fastest human being ever timed, with a list of world records as long as his magnificent, striding legs. At the Rio 2016 games Bolt won gold in the 100 metres, the 200 metres and the 4x100-metre relay. That meant he'd earned three gold medals at three consecutive Olympics and completed a "triple-triple". Truly a living legend.

THE FASTEST 100M SPRINT ON RECORD

▶ Senior Moment

https://youtu.be/50zgKD_xN-A

If you think most septuagenarians drive at the speed of an ice cream van you should check out George Poteet. Legendary hot-rod racer George has gone faster than 400 mph (644 km/h) more than 50 times, while setting over 20 land speed records, but he lost his (piston engine) land speed record in 2018. Two years later, at the age of 72, he was determined to win it back. On the famed Bonneville salt flats, he settled into the "Speed Demon", a golden 32-foot (9.8-metre) rocket-shaped car, put his foot down and registered a two-way average speed of 470 mph (756 km/h) – smashing the record by over 20 mph (32 km/h).

▼ Splash Dash

http://y2u.be/sAubG28uODM

As speed records go, driving at 54 mph (87 km/h) isn't very fast. Except Gudbjørn Grimsson is driving on water. In an extreme Formula Offroad race in Iceland, the local driver took his suitably named Insane Racing buggy through the mud and drove over 1,000 feet (300 metres) down the river. With huge-treaded tyres acting like scoops on a paddle steamer, the buggy skims along on the water. To generate enough power, the car has four-wheel drive and a 1,600 horsepower twin-turbo engine. So probably best not to try it in the family estate car then.

THE FASTEST CAR ON WATER

▼ Striking Distance

https://youtu.be/Spmp3S4QPQM

Athletes had to make the most of every event in a Covid-19-disrupted 2020 season. Ugandan runner Joshua Cheptegei certainly did that. He broke world records in each of his three outings in the year. In February he became the first man ever to run a 3.1-mile (5 km) road race in less than 13 minutes; in August he broke a 16-year record at the same distance on the track; and then in October he capped a sensational year by smashing the 15-year-old 10,000 metres track record. As Mo Farah's career drew to a close, distance running had undoubtedly found a new hero.

Solar Power

https://youtu.be/ZAD3CNWrM98

Launched in 2018, the Parker Solar Probe, NASA's mission to 'touch the Sun', uses Venus' gravity over a series of flybys to bring its orbit closer to the Sun. In April 2021, the probe flew at around 330,000 miles per hour (532,000 kph), the fastest ever speed achieved by a human-made object, which took it within 6.5 million miles (10.4 million kilometres) of the Sun – the closest we have ever been. As every pass brings it nearer to the solar surface and increases the probe's speed, it will continue to break its own record until the end of its mission in late 2025.

EXTREME WEATHER

Witness the shock and devastation brought by these record-breaking natural disasters – hurricanes, tsunamis and other calamitous events – in tense and dramatic footage uploaded to YouTube.

▼ Weather Report

http://y2u.be/unV5KcSrY-I

This clip went viral and became known as the "Hurricane Charley Gas Station" video. It shows a petrol station in Charlotte Harbor, Florida, being torn apart by winds of over 155 mph (249 km/h). Hurricane Charley, classed as Category 4 (the second strongest band), was the strongest hurricane to hit southwest Florida for 50 years. These winds were the strongest ever caught on video and were captured by Mike Theiss, whose brilliant weather films appear on the Ultimate Chase channel.

The Super Tsunami

http://y2u.be/2uCZjqoRLjc

On 9 July 1958, an earthquake caused a landslide at the head of Lituya Bay in Alaska. It generated a mega-tsunami measuring between 100 feet (30 metres) and 300 feet (91 metres), the highest tsunami wave in recorded history. This fascinating four-minute BBC clip tells the story of the tsunami, illuminated by the work of scientists who have uncovered evidence of the destruction caused. It has been viewed more than two million times.

▶ Stone Me

https://youtu.be/_IUnxt0fFV8

Hailstones are lumps of ice that form in the clouds and fall to the ground when they become too heavy. This normally occurs when they reach 0.2 inches (5mm) in diameter. However, hailstones are formed in volatile thunder clouds and strong up-drafts can mean that instead of falling they are carried up to the freezing top of the cloud and enlarged. On 8 February 2018, a freak 20-minute hailstorm battered towns in Cordoba, Argentina, with hailstones that caused holes in the ground, damaged houses and deposited one incredible record-breaking hailstone that measured 9 inches (23 centimetres).

THE LARGEST LANDSLIDE IN HISTORY

▲ Mount Devastation

http://y2u.be/IhU6jml6NY4

Mount St Helens is a volcano in the US state of Washington. In 1980, an earthquake caused the north face to slide away, creating the largest landslide ever recorded. The landslide triggered explosions that sent rocks, ash, volcanic gas and steam into the air at over 300 mph (483 km/h) and created a column of ash that reached more than 15 miles (24 kilometres) into the atmosphere in only 15 minutes. This video, created from a series of photographs, reveals the enormity of this colossal act of nature.

AMAZING ANIMAL RECORDS

The animal kingdom has its champions too. A safari through YouTube's wildlife clips reveals some fascinating and surprising records and some incredible footage from the wild world.

▶ Monkey Business

http://y2u.be/zsXP8qeFF6A

About 98 per cent of their genome is identical to humans, so it is not surprising that chimpanzees are regarded as the cleverest of animal species. They can make and use tools, hunt in organized groups and have shown they are capable of empathy, altruism and self-awareness. Over and above all this, they are adept at computer skills – and in the case of Ayumu, featured in this video, can beat a human at memory games.

CHIMP WITH A MEMORY SUPERIOR TO HUMANS

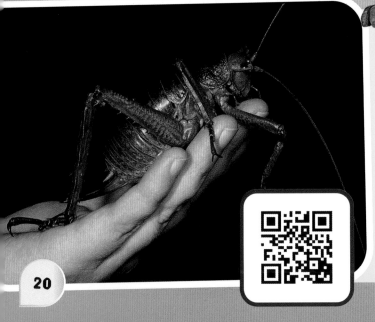

◀ Big Bug

http://y2u.be/tBaRwtzFBbo

The Maoris call it "the God of Ugly Things". Bit rude? Looking at a picture of the Giant Weta, you might think it's a little like a cricket and not really that unsightly, but see the insect in real life and – whoa! – it's the size of a rodent. Once common in New Zealand, the world's biggest insect is now believed to live only on Little Barrier Island, about 50 miles (80 km) northeast of Auckland. Weighing more than a sparrow, this creature is too heavy to jump, let alone fly, but it can pack a nasty nip with its oversized pincers.

▼ Small Wonder

https://youtu.be/FcJrQ9pUq5k

Between 3 and 5 feet (1 and 1.5 metres) high and 6 to 13 feet (2 to 4 metres) long, Sumatran rhinos are the smallest – and as you'll see here, the absolute cutest – surviving species of rhinoceros. Covered with hair they are, according to the WWF, more closely related to the extinct woolly rhinos than any of the other living rhino species. Once found in their thousands across South East Asia, they are now one of the most critically endangered species on the planet. There are believed to be less than 80 still alive in the wild on the Indonesian islands of Sumatra and Borneo.

▶ Loud Hailer

https://youtu.be/dvK-DujvpSY

This video has an on-screen warning that advises you to move your headphones away from your ears. That's because this is the white bellbird. It lives in the mountains of northeastern South America and it holds the record for the bird with the loudest call. The sound reverberates like a bell and is created by the male, who is pure white. This noisy creature has a wattle that wobbles when he warbles, and when he opens his beak, the volume hits 125 decibels, which is as loud as a pneumatic drill.

CUTEST RHINO EVER

◀ Short Shark Shock

https://youtu.be/8raLJHzWqVA

Deep Blue is a real life Jaws. At 20 feet (6 metres) long, she's thought to be the largest great white shark ever caught on film and the 50-year-old beast (they can live past 70) was filmed by diving enthusiast Michael Maier off the coast of Guadalupe Island, Mexico. Now, shark attacks are rare, but if you're going to suffer an aquatic assault it is most likely to be at the teeth of a great white – so how brave is the guy in the diving suit who goes for a high five with the marvellous marauding creature?

FREAKY FOOD RECORDS

The world of food and drink showcases some marvellous records, including enormous vegetables, oversized fast food and a time-honoured crazy method of cracking open champagne bottles.

▶ Death on the Menu

https://youtu.be/tsqOJJATl0k

Imagine going to a restaurant and ordering a dish that is 200 times more deadly than cyanide and can kill you in hours? The death is horrible: you are paralysed and slowly suffocate while remaining conscious to the end. Fugu or pufferfish, whose organs contain the neurotoxin tetrodotoxin, are the most poisonous food in the world and yet are commonly eaten in restaurants in Japan and China. This is because when prepared by a licensed and highly skilled chef the fish is perfectly safe – and delicious, if very expensive. Nevertheless, deaths are regularly recorded: mainly anglers who attempt to eat their own catch. I'll just have the fries, thanks.

Grim Reaper

http://y2u.be/3zhym9oUSGU

The "Carolina Reaper", a crossbreed between a Ghost chilli pepper and a Red Habanero pepper, has been rated as the world's hottest chilli pepper. It averages 1,569,300 on the Scoville scale, making it over 900 times hotter than Tabasco sauce. There are enough chilli-eating videos on YouTube to show what excruciating results can occur, but despite that the Danish TV host, Bubber, is foolish enough to step up to the plate...

Wotzilla

https://youtu.be/IwyYRCvIS9o

In January 2020, Walkers brought out "Wotsit Giants", which are twice the size of normal Wotsits. But for some, that still wasn't big enough, so a team from the factory in Leicester produced a monster Cheesy Wotsit – the longest puffed corn snack on the planet – and called it "Wotzilla". Although the same width as a normal Wotsit Giant, Wotzilla was 35 feet (10.66 metres) long, equivalent in length to 164 regular Wotsit Giants and weighed 0.5 pounds (250 grams). Unfortunately, though, its makers didn't get to enjoy the massive snack – a Walkers spokesman said, "We're going to get it mounted and display it on the wall at the factory!"

◀ Raising the Bar

https://youtu.be/G_kgVLhCCrA

The Snickers bar has long been a favourite among chocoholics, but surely even they couldn't dream of tucking into a bar this big. In January 2020, a 12-foot (3.5-metre) long, 2-foot (0.9-metre) high and 26-inch (0.6-metre) wide Snickers bar was unveiled. Weighing in at 4,700 pounds (2,132 kilograms), it was the size of 43,000 normal bars – that's 12 million calories! Looking and tasting just like the real thing with layers of nougat, peanut and caramel coated in milk chocolate, it was made in the Mars Wrigley factory in Waco, Texas, and took a week to produce. Well, they do say everything is bigger in Texas!

Gold Plated

https://youtu.be/1C3oTE0Px90

It's always good to try a new food, right, so native New Yorker Casey Neistat sets out to sample the speciality of Ainsworth's, a restaurant just a few blocks from his office. The dish may well be mouth-watering and it certainly comes with an eye-watering price tag of a thousand bucks. What is it? Chicken wings, but not just any old chicken wings. These chicken wings are coated and fried in genuine 24-carat gold dust. So do the wings pass the taste test for Casey and his friend Sean? Pull a chair up and watch.

RECORD-BREAKING PEOPLE

Those born at the extremes of the physical spectrum – the tallest, the smallest, etc. – have always held a special fascination. These clips reveal the human beings behind some of the statistics.

Bite-Sized

https://youtu.be/aSS3BVFNDQo

Seeing the huge cavern that appears when Phillip Angus opens his mouth wide – it's big enough to fit a tin of beans with ease – it's a wonder it didn't dawn on him sooner that he was a record-breaker. However, the 16-year-old from Pennsylvania, USA, only realized he had a large mouth when he tried to pop his ears, after having trouble hearing. He checked YouTube for the world record for the largest gape and measured his own at a whopping 3.75 inches (9.52 centimetres). He beat the old record by more than a quarter of an inch (0.6 centimetres), which left him, well, open-mouthed.

THE WORLD'S TALLEST TEENAGER

 ## ▶ Tall Story

https://youtu.be/qi7f1F2tcGE

Sometimes being a physical record holder can be a burden. Some are bullied or seen as freaks, but the world's tallest teen, Olivier Rioux from Montreal, has taken advantage of his status on the basketball court. Oliver stands at seven foot, five inches (2.26 metres) tall and he is only 15 years old, so he has four more years to break his own record. But his ambitions lie elsewhere. Olivier has played basketball for Canada at the U16 Americas Championship (pictured), trained with Real Madrid in Spain and joined the prestigious IMG Academy in Florida. It's no lie that for this tall teen the sky's the limit!

◀ Animal Magnetism

http://y2u.be/rbUuzCRa3Ug

Former kick-boxing coach Etibar Elchyev from Georgia is known as "Magnetic Man". Ever since he discovered his ability to attract metal objects to his body, Etibar has been setting new records. Here, in December 2013, we find him putting spoons on his chest and back – 53 in total, a new world record. An excellent talent, but he must dread visiting the cafeteria. Scientists claim his skin is not magnetic but merely "sticky". Whatever ... he's still in a magnetic field of his own!

THE MOST SPOONS ON A HUMAN BODY

▶ Inseparable Brothers

http://y2u.be/gPcijt2WaIs

Twin brothers Ronnie and Donnie Galyon were born healthy in Dayton, Ohio, in October 1951. Joined at the waist, they each had arms, legs and separate hearts but shared a stomach and some organs. Sixty-three years later they were still joined and could celebrate being the oldest-ever conjoined twins, beating Italian brothers Giacomo and Giovanni Battista Tocci, who were born in 1877. The twins spent their lives from the age of four in circus sideshows but have now retired to live with their younger brother.

THE LONGEST-LIVING CONJOINED TWINS IN THE WORLD

WILD AND WACKY

Hidden away in the nooks and corners of YouTube are some odd and eccentric records. Here are just a few ...

◢ Living Doll

http://y2u.be/mhcW_81GRsU

Now aged 33, Brazilian-born Briton Jessica (formerly Rodrigo) Alves has been having cosmetic surgery for over 15 years. She has had 51 surgeries and more than 100 cosmetic procedures – an official world record – and has completely changed his appearance. Her nickname is "Human Ken" (after Barbie's boyfriend), and she most recently underwent a CO_2 laser treatment that burned off the top layer of her skin to leave her with a porcelain-like, blemish-free complexion. Alves, who is set to appear in a TV series about real-life dolls, says she has no intention of stopping and plans even more cosmetic changes.

THE WORLD'S MOST DOLL-LIKE HuMAN

Lego Torture

https://youtu.be/m6xowlcxYGA

"I hope you step on a Lego" is a modern-day curse used in hundreds of memes. The pain of stepping on one of the plastic bricks is not easily forgotten, so walking barefoot over a lego-strewn path is on a par with traversing red hot coals and best left to the experts. Step forward (cautiously) Salacnib "Sonny" Molina, owner of five world records for barefoot running. Admittedly, the hour-long video of his record-breaking 3.1-mile (5 km) walk back and forth across a tray of bricks may become slightly dull after a while, but fast-forward to the end and see the state of his feet when he finishes. Ouch, ouch, ouch!

◄ Tattoo Love

http://y2u.be/QIULSyKIrGY

Couples need a shared interest and there's no prize for guessing Chuck Helmke and Charlotte Guttenberg's common passion. Chuck, aged 75, and Charlotte, a sprightly 65-year-old, met in a tattoo studio in 2006. Charlotte was just discovering the joys of body art, while Chuck had begun covering his body in ink five years earlier. Now they are officially the male and female most-tattooed senior citizens world record holders. Displaying a colourful array of intricate tattoos, both boast over 90 per cent body coverage, with even their shaved heads inked. There's not a lot anyone can do to beat that!

MOST-TATTOOED SENIOR CITIZENS

▶ Dead Cool

http://y2u.be/xtHzRjnoXKw

In November 2014 in Mexico City, 509 slightly scary-looking skeletons in ball gowns and brimmed hats gathered in the city centre to set the world record for the largest gathering of Catrinas. The figure of Catrina, known as the Elegant Death, was created and immortalized in works by artists Guadalupe Posada and Diego Rivera and is now a traditional part of Mexico's Day of the Dead celebrations. People dress as the skeletal character to visit cemeteries and share offerings and food with the dead and their families.

A RECORD GATHERING OF CATRINAS

27

SPORTS RECORD BREAKERS

There's more to sport than winning. There are records to be broken. These athletes have etched their names in the history of their sports – however strange!

▼ All in a Day's Work

http://y2u.be/CQIk-aAHhFY

These days, breaking a record is as much about producing a great YouTube video as it is about performing the feat. The Face Team Acrobatic Sports Theatre of Hungary have certainly grasped that fact. They broke five world records in one day – the most basketball slam dunks by a team using a trampoline in one minute; the highest throw and catch of a spinning basketball; the farthest forward flip trampette slam dunk; the longest time spinning a basketball on a guitar; and the most passes of a spinning basketball in one minute (pair) – and captured it all in a fun three-minute video. Perfect.

Fin-tastic!

https://youtu.be/Yc6G_pjma5k

'He leapt like a salmon' is a phrase sports commentators reserve for a slam dunk in basketball or a header in football, but it has never been as apt as it is for this feat by Egyptian swimmer Omar Sayed Shaaban. One of the world's fastest underwater sprinters, Omar turned his attentions to above the water line as he recorded a world record for the highest jump from water wearing a monofin (a single fin fitting over both feet). Using all of the flexibility and strong leg muscles built up in his training, he leapt an incredible 7.5 feet (2.3 metres) out of the water.

BEST LEAPING BASKET-BALLERS

▶ Goal Machine

https://youtu.be/YFVCOev7uYw

When you think of the highest-scoring international footballers, names such as Ali Daei and Cristiano Ronaldo, or Mia Hamm or Marta, come to mind. Canada's Christine Sinclair might be less well-known, but she beats them all by a long way, having notched her 185th goal against St Kitts and Nevis in an Olympic qualifying match in February 2020. Sinclair is a phenomenal goal hunter and poacher, with a ratio of a goal every 1.5 games. She is an inspiration to millions of young players and thoroughly deserves her place among the world's greats.

Hopping Mad!

https://youtu.be/L0nRle2oN54

The pogo stick has been a children's favourite for 80 years or so, but it only became the instrument of an extreme sport at the turn of the century. Supercharged springs and lightweight frames have made it a hopping cousin to the skateboard and BMX, and the annual competition, Pogopalooza, which started in 2004, now attracts thousands of fans and the world's best pogoers. That's where the high jump world record is usually smashed, but this video features Biff Hutchison (who has broken multiple bones in his body coming off his stick) taking the prize in his own backyard. He cleared a bar set at an incredible 11 feet and half an inch (3.35 metres) high!

▶ Clogged Up

http://y2u.be/2CdYF41M6rw

Australian Rugby Union hero Drew Mitchell is his country's highest World Cup try scorer. However, the Toulon winger, who has played over 70 times for Australia, is also a serial record breaker. On the Sky Sports Rugby TV channel, he became joint holder of the records for both the most rugby passes and the most drop goals in a minute. He then set the record for the most apples crushed with the bicep in one minute (it was 14) and went on to perform this intriguing feat: the fastest 100 metres in clogs. Wearing the heavy, wooden, Klomp-style clog common to the Netherlands, Drew hit the finish line in just 14.43 seconds.

FASTEST 100M WEARING CLOGS

THEME PARK RECORDS

Scream if you want to go faster! Actually, it isn't possible to go any faster than on some of these record-breaking rides – but you may find yourself screaming anyway.

FASTEST, LONGEST, TALLEST DIVE COASTER

▼ Gee Force

http://y2u.be/N79JKDtK4hg

What is it with you people? Sixteen million views? It's just a ride! The Zumanjaro: Drop of Doom, at the Six Flags Great Adventure in New Jersey, USA, is the tallest and fastest drop ride in the world. The eight-person gondola speeds to the top of the 415-foot (126-metre) structure in about 30 seconds, leaves them there a while to enjoy the view (or just exchange some nervous giggles) before rocketing them back down at 90 mph (145 km/h), reaching ground level again in less than 10 seconds – before they even have time to scream.

Twist and Shout

https://youtu.be/V5rJVPSSoFs

Yukon Striker, which opened at Canada's Wonderland in Ontario in 2019, is 223 feet (68 metres) high, 3,625 feet (1,105 metres) long and has a maximum speed of 81 mph (130 km/h). It also has a 90-degree drop and four inversions, including a complete 360-degree loop, all of which makes it the world's tallest, longest and fastest dive coaster (a type of rollercoaster featuring a near-vertical drop). For maximum effect watch this POV video full screen, but to be on the safe side don't eat first!

THE WORLD'S FASTEST DROP RIDE

▼ Slippery Slope

https://youtu.be/exxcazMTzAk

At least on YouTube you can enjoy this one without getting wet or worrying about drowning at the end. At just under 164 feet (50 metres), the Kilimanjaro water slide is the tallest body slide (one that doesn't require a raft) in the world. The slide at the Águas Quentes Country Club outside Rio de Janeiro, Brazil, takes a terrifying 60-foot (18-metre) drop into the pool way below. Apparently, nearly a third of those who reach the entrance are not brave enough to take the plunge, but those who do achieve speeds of over 60 mph (100 km/h).

Fast Formula

http://y2u.be/ijuQwnfBBZw

The Formula Rossa rollercoaster in Abu Dhabi's Ferrari World boasts acceleration from 0 to 60 mph (96 km/h) in just two seconds and reaches a world record 149 mph (240 km/h). In 2010, Felipe Massa and Fernando Alonso, Formula One motor-racing drivers, took their seats in the fastest rollercoaster on the planet. Now, while their bodies are used to being flung around at ridiculously high speeds, their faces are usually encased in helmets. Just watch as the G-force hits these seasoned speed merchants.

COULD YOU BRAVE THE WORLD'S TALLEST WATER SLIDE?

SCARY AND SHOCKING!

Delve into the lucky dip of the world of records and who knows what'll emerge. You could find some hair-raising danger, interesting collections and, sometimes, something truly, truly bizarre.

SUPERCAR UP A SUPER MOUNTAIN

BORDER ROADS ORGANISATION
KHARDUNGLA TOP
(18380 FEET)
HIGHEST MOTORABLE ROAD IN THE WORLD
54RCC   HIMANK   16 TF

▲ Take the High Road

https://youtu.be/ZVwy7knb1F0

Local signs claim Khardung La is the top of the world and host to "the highest motorable road on earth". Situated in the Himalayas in Northern India, the road climbs from 15,000 feet (3,500 metres) up to 18,000 feet (5,600 metres) in just a few hours' drive, with both the altitude change and the views leaving travellers breathless. *Autocar India*'s Nikhil Bhatia decides to see just how "motorable" the road is by taking a Lamborghini Huracan up its slopes. As the road gets rockier and narrower, with vertical drops awaiting those who veer off the track, it is super-mountain versus supercar all the way to the top.

▼ Bridge Too Far?

https://youtu.be/Vhni_I4Ld0Y

It's very windy up on Ai-Petri, a peak in the Ukraine's Crimean Mountains, and it's also pretty foggy. However, you can take the cable car to the top and from there you can cross from rocky outcrop to rocky outcrop on a series of simple suspension bridges. No doubt walking through the clouds is an exhilarating experience, but the construction does look rather rickety – it's just a lot of short planks strung together with ropes for rails. Could this be the scariest set of bridges in the world?

Walk the Plank

http://y2u.be/KbtZfzxX44o

How far are you prepared to go for a breathtaking view? If you would happily walk along a seemingly rickety plank attached to the side of a mountain cliff hundreds of feet high, then Mount Huashan in China could be your ideal destination. The plankway doesn't lead anywhere – just to a stunning bird's-eye view of the surrounding mountains – and you have to return the same way, negotiating your way past those coming in the opposite direction. Overcome your fears, though, and you, too, can claim to have taken the world's most dangerous hiking trail.

Human Fireball

http://y2u.be/hICWU9HC7ts

Fire-protective clothing is available, as worn by motor-racing drivers and movie stunt men. It's not for Anthony Britton, though. He dressed himself in three pairs of overalls, a few balaclavas and a motorcycle helmet for his attempt on the world record for fire running. Hundreds of spectators assembled in a park in Croydon, England, to watch Anthony, an experienced escapologist, soak himself in petrol, set himself on fire and run hell for leather across the grass. He completed an awesome 595 feet (181 metres) before calling in his team to douse the flames with fire extinguishers.

▶ Blown Away

http://y2u.be/AdtSdVop6V0

The James Bond franchise of movies has a long history of breaking a plethora of records. However, this achievement is arguably the most earth-shattering of them all. The climax of *Spectre*, the 24th Bond film in the series, featured the largest film-stunt explosion ever as Blofeld's desert base was detonated to kingdom come in front of the film's stars, Daniel Craig and Madeleine Swann. Shot on 29 June 2015 in Erfoud, Morocco, the blast used 2,224 gallons (10,110 litres) of fuel and 73 pounds (33 kilograms) of explosives. The sequence might have lasted just seven and a half seconds, but it was one memorable blast.

DON'T TRY THIS AT HOME!

How desperate can you be to get your name in the record books? These record breakers seem to feel no pain as they take one or more of their senses to the limit.

Candles in the Wind

http://y2u.be/kvGa-OXORhw

It's not big and it's not clever – though you have to admit it is kind of cool. File this in the not-to-try-at-home folder, but do take a look at 28-year-old Filipino Ronald Cabañas extinguishing five lit candles with his own bottom wind. In an extraordinary display of controlled flatulence, Ronald, using what can only be described as a home-made fart trumpet, puts out the candles in less than 30 seconds. It is a fine skill, but it's difficult to see how Ronald, a farmer and sometime porter, can make a career of it.

▶ Peg Face

http://y2u.be/pS2AszO0z44

GREATEST NUMBER OF PEGS ON FACE

We've all got a skill lurking somewhere, it's just a matter of finding it. Kelvin "The Peg Man" Mercado, 36 years old, discovered he had a unique talent for clipping clothes pegs on his face. Now he's a world-record holder. Pegs are attached in neat formation to every loose, and not so loose, piece of skin as well as to his lips and nose. Altogether he managed to clip on 163 pegs – and it makes for quite a sight.

34

In Full Swing

https://youtu.be/rXpJjdXUq9c

Inspired by the nunchuck skills of actor Bruce Lee in his kung-fu movies, Xie Desheng from Shanghai has become a master of the chain-sticks weapon. Fighting and acting are not for Xie, though. He demonstrates his unerring accuracy with the nunchucks with breathtaking exhibitions of skill. So far he has amassed five world records, including removing 10 bottle caps, extinguishing 52 candles in a minute and hitting 32 ping-pong balls with his deadly weapon, all within 60 seconds. His latest entry in the record books is this staggering display where he lights 21 matches in a minute as they are held out by very trusting fingers.

▼ Riding High

https://youtu.be/Pn0Tyqwr7To

"One of the best things we've ever had on *Britain's Got Talent*," said David Walliams, and it was indeed an incredible performance. American unicyclist Wesley Williams thrilled Simon Cowell and the judges, and had the audience on the edge of their seats as he rode his unicycle up a set of stairs and then juggled several knives while balancing on the tall bike. But they screamed with horror – so much so that hosts Ant and Dec had to warn them to keep silent to aid his concentration – as he mounted a world record 22-foot (6.7-metre) high unicycle…

▶ Fired Up

https://youtu.be/WQT1IVUrO2s

Bryan Miser is a human cannonball and the record-breaking "Human Fuse". Not only is he shot from a canon to land – with any luck – on a large inflatable, but as part of this process he is also set alight. This is Bryan's 2019 audition for *America's Got Talent* and as he flies through the air in flames you can really feel the tension. The audience were open-mouthed, but what do you think Simon Cowell and the other judges had to say?

THIRST-QUENCHING RECORDS

It's not just drinking the liquid stuff quickly (although, boy, can they guzzle!), but shaking it, sucking it, carrying it and performing all sorts of records with it!

Beer Duty

http://y2u.be/nALw8IOLDfw

Tax inspector by day, tankard carrier by beer festival, Oliver Strümpfel is a superhero in the bar-tending world. His personal arena is the Gillamoos Fair in Abensberg, Bavaria, where he is king of the *Maßkrugtragen* – the beer-stein carrying challenge. He took up the challenge to try to beat an Australian who reigned as the Meister of *Maßkrugtragen*. In 2010 he managed to beat him by carrying 21 tankards. In 2014 he took his record to 25. Following a nine-month gym regime, this is Strümpfel's 2017 attempt to extend his record even further.

Chug a Lug

https://youtu.be/x0f2mcgNUIk

Eric 'Badlands' Booker is a professional eater, rapper, and chugging specialist. He has a real talent for consuming fizzy liquids at top speed, but how quickly can he suck up five cans of delicious cranberry-flavoured Sprite? Well, it takes him longer to fill the large glass boot with his favourite soft drink than it does to down it, and his burp lasts almost as long as the chug itself, but it's a world record (at least, according to Eric it is) and certainly pretty impressive.

▶ Flip Out

http://y2u.be/lNb2FChnoIQ

As 2017 began, bottle-flipping had reached epidemic proportions. Kids everywhere were flicking a partially filled plastic bottle in the hope it would land on its base. Schools banned the practice and Mike Senatore, the man whose viral video had launched the craze, went online to apologise for distracting the nation's youth. Out in Sweden, things became even crazier. With a 28.5-gallon (130 litre) bottle supplied by supermarket chain Lidl, two YouTubers ventured to the middle of a bridge to attempt the world's biggest bottle flip...

CHAMPION BOTTLE-FLIPPER

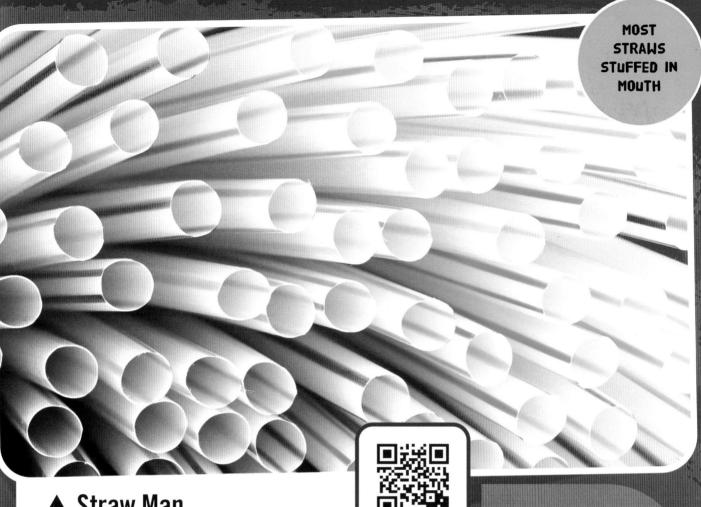

▲ Straw Man

http://y2u.be/15BCllVcz38

As a child, Manoj Kumar Maharana dreamed of breaking a world record and, finally, as a 23-year-old, he fulfilled his ambition. He could have set out to win the Olympic 100 Metres or lift a car above his head, but instead he decided to beat Simon Elmore, a Brit who crammed 400 straws in his mouth in 2009. In 2017, Manoj managed to stuff an amazing 459 plastic drinking straws into his mouth at once, successfully keeping them there for the requisite 10 seconds without touching them.

▼ Milking It

http://y2u.be/kBFugzV1KxI

Kobayashi shows his awesome power of consumption. Here he is at Uncle Bob's Self Storage in Upper Saddle River, New Jersey, tipping one gallon (4.5 litres) – of milk down his gullet in just 20 seconds. According to the clip's description, Kobayashi had set a record of eating 13 cupcakes in a minute, "so he needed to wash it down". Considering human stomachs are said to be able to contain around 6 pints (3.4 litres), it's difficult to imagine where it is all going.

Human Hydrant

http://y2u.be/U9_JFjZGkYA

There are over 600 muscles in the human body and many of them can be utilised to break a world record. Take Kirubel Yilma of Addis Ababa for example. He's a medical student who put his knowledge of anatomy to use to achieve a record for spraying water from the mouth. He beat the existing record by 10 seconds as he squirted a continuous spray of water from his mouth for nearly a minute!

THE BIGGEST!

When it comes to record breaking, size is definitely important. The Biggest … is always one of the most popular of the records categories. Here are a few colossal contributors …

Pricey Pyrotechnics

https://youtu.be/erQ_9yEz0ls

To regular YouTube viewers, Mr Beast needs no introduction. His channel has 50 million subscribers and his most popular videos, such as "I put 100 million orbeez in my friend's backyard" or "Going through the same drive-thru 1,000 times" have earned around 100 million views. Mr Beast likes to go big and go expensive, so when his focus turned to fireworks, viewers knew what to expect. Out in the wilds, Mr Beast and his friends run through increasingly expensive rockets, firecrackers and explosions until they reach the pinnacle: the world's biggest firework, a massive multi-mortar weighing 4,000 pounds (1,814 kilograms). It cost him $160,000, but did the big spender get the bang for his buck?

WORLD'S LARGEST BOWL OF CEREAL

▶ Cereal Killer

https://youtu.be/xRwy_rKc7gl

This challenge is much tougher than you might think and it starts with the world's largest cereal bowl, which is filled with 2,000 gallons (9,092 litres) of water, a lot of milk powder, and boxes and boxes of out-of-date breakfast cereal. It also involves cartoon creature costumes, rubber rings and four random members of the public. Whoever stays in the cereal bowl the longest wins $10,000. There's a great moment (among many) when one of the participants, running low on willpower and energy, asks for a granola bar.

He's Got a Nerf

https://youtu.be/DyRwWyWUtjY

Nerf blasters have been around since the 1990s. They shoot foam darts at a speed that is enough to create an impression, but not to hurt. So far, so sensible. Then along came inventors like Michael Pick who have taken the Nerf gun idea to a whole new level. His 12.5-foot (3.8-metre) long replica – the world's largest Nerf gun – is 300 times as big as the original, weighs over 200 pounds (90 kilos) and propels darts via a paintball air tank. His foam-covered PVC darts fly as far as 250 feet (76 metres) and can demolish a breeze block. Just hope your little brother doesn't get one for Christmas!

▼ Off the Wall

http://y2u.be/EptwF6cZMWg

Of all the records set in Brazil's Olympic year, this is the most eye-catching. Artist Eduardo Kobra designed a huge mural called *Etnias*, meaning "Ethnicities", on a wall of the Olympic Boulevard in Rio de Janeiro. The colourful spray-painted mural depicts the faces of indigenous people from five different continents. Using 180 buckets of acrylic paint and 3,500 cans of spray paint, the painting stands 51 feet (15.5 metres) high and stretches for 560 feet (170 metres). It's the largest spray-painted mural in the world, and it took Kobra and his team two months to complete.

THE WORLD'S BIGGEST MURAL

THE MORE, THE MERRIER!

Ah, mass participation! A chance to meet other bizarrely dressed folk, to stretch your legs in unison or to smack each other around the head with a pillow!

▲ Pillow Talk

http://y2u.be/KQ_SYl9vlkc

Nobody wants to see fighting at a sports stadium, but maybe we can make an exception for CHS Field, the home of Minnesota baseball team St Paul Saints. At the end of the second inning of the Saints' match against the Winnipeg Goldeyes, a battle broke out – among all 6,261 of the spectators. This was a mass display of that friendliest of confrontations – the pillow fight. Provided with weapons by a local pillow company, the crowd, staff and mascots (although sadly not the players) attacked their neighbours with their night-time bolsters. It was the biggest pillow fight in the world – ever!

▼ Zombie Apocalypse (almost)

http://y2u.be/QkqC6Fni2KE

They bill the Zombie Pub Crawl as the World's Greatest Undead Party with brain-eating competitions, live pop acts, a "Trapped in the Closet Sing-Along" and a zombie fun run! Minneapolis has been hosting the living dead (or people dressed up as them) annually since 2005. The original 500 zombies have multiplied until, in 2014, over 15,000 people were officially counted stumbling around in a stupefied manner. It was the official record for a zombie gathering.

RECORD-BREAKING NUMBER OF ZOMBIES

▶ Under Attack

https://youtu.be/DCGDqQxmUDM

At Comic-Con in San Diego, California, in July 2019, fans of the Japanese anime TV series *Dragon Ball Z* set out to smash the world record for the largest number of people to perform the kamehameha (pronounced kah-may-ha-may-ha). The kamehameha is the first super energy attack – what you might call the signature move of the character Goku – and the previous record was 250. Fortunately, actor Sean Schemmel, who voices Goku, was on hand to warm up the 784-strong crowd and teach them how to get it just right.

◀ Packed Pillion

http://y2u.be/YwRafRr8dk4

The Indian Army has set a new world record for 58 men riding on a single motorbike. It's not a skill modern soldiers should need but, with defence-budget cuts common, you never know. The 500-cc Royal Enfield chugged along an Air Force runway and covered a distance of 0.75 miles (1.2 kilometres) with members of the Tornadoes, an army motorcycle display team, precariously balancing on either side. The stunt, which broke the Tornadoes' own record by four riders, involved six months' planning and training, military discipline and precision – and quite a lot of falling off.

MOST PEOPLE RIDING A SINGLE MOTORBIKE

Dance Craze

https://youtu.be/E5YEVURAeRM

Even though much of the world was still sheltering from the Coronavirus pandemic, the Jerusalema Challenge was big in the summer of 2020. The challenge was to perform a dance to the song 'Jerusalema', a gospel-influenced house track performed by South African singer-songwriter Nomcebo. Versions of the dance – a combination of butt-waggling and simple steps – were posted from around the world, including from the Swiss and Irish police forces, but mainly the dancers gyrated in groups of four and five. Fittingly, it was South Africa that took it to extremes, with over 600 people turning up to dance in the coastal town of Plettenberg Bay.

WILD WEATHER RECORDS

Mother Nature is a prodigious record breaker and produces some of the most spectacular events you can see on YouTube. Just watch the disintegrating iceberg, dramatic twister and other gripping footage on these pages.

Tip of the Iceberg

http://y2u.be/hC3VTglPoGU

Over 20 million people have watched this amazing clip from the documentary *Chasing Ice*. The footage shows the historic breakup at the Ilulissat Glacier in western Greenland – the largest iceberg calving ever filmed. Glacial calving happens when an iceberg breaks off from the larger ice shelf, in this case a piece measuring 1.8 cubic miles (7.4 cubic km). The Ilulissat (aka Jakobshavn) glacier produces around 10 per cent of all Greenland icebergs with around 35 billion tons of icebergs calving off every year.

▼ The Heat is On

https://youtu.be/IMDN5s9CnPI

The name of the location gives you a good clue: Furnace Creek, Death Valley, Mojave Desert, California. It gets hot there. Very hot. And on 16 August 2020 it officially became the hottest place on record as temperatures soared to 130 degrees Fahrenheit (54.4 degrees Celsius). Those who live and work in the desert are used to extreme temperatures, but this was something else. Being outside was like stepping into an oven and they had to constantly sip water and avoid touching metal, because it burned the skin. Experts warn that as the effects of global warming take hold, this is a record that will be broken again and again.

RECORD-BREAKING LIGHTNING STORMS

▲ Everlasting Lightning

http://y2u.be/edrAL2t99kE

In 2014, an area of northwestern Venezuela, where the Catatumbo River meets Lake Maracaibo, was officially recognized as having the most frequent lightning storms. Known as "Relámpago del Catatumbo" – "the Catatumbo Lightning" – this "everlasting storm" appears almost every night. Averaging 28 lightning strikes per minute for up to 10 hours at a time, it can spark as many as 3,600 bolts in an hour. Although many myths surround the phenomenon, scientists claim it is just regular lightning, whose frequency can be explained by regional topography and wind patterns.

Chillsville, Siberia

http://y2u.be/gRbaAaJgW0A

Next time you feel a little chilly, spare a thought for the 500 or so inhabitants of Oymyakon, the coldest inhabited place on Earth. Oymyakon (the name ironically means "unfrozen water") is in northeastern Siberia, a two-day drive from the world's coldest major city, Yakutsk, and just a few hundred miles from the Arctic Circle. It is pitch-black dark for up to 21 hours a day during the winter and the temperature averages -50° Celsius (-58° Fahrenheit). In 1933, it plunged to -68°C (-90°F). Get through that, though, and you can look forward to endless summer days and temperatures rising to a balmy 23°Celsius (73°F).

Haven't the Foggiest

https://youtu.be/nOfMTOj1wNc

Is Lark Harbour, a small fishing community on the western coast of the Canadian province of Newfoundland, the foggiest place in the world? It must surely be one of them, because when the fog rolls in from the sea it's like an enormous waterfall or an avalanche of fog. This video is shot looking up at the wall of fog, and it's cool but slightly scary. However, do click the link above to the video taken from further away, because that's awesome too.

EXTREME SPORTS RECORDS

There's danger out there on the streets. Especially if you are mad enough to try to go faster, higher, lower than anyone else in your chosen extreme sport.

Sacré Bleu!

http://y2u.be/MV2iURlttxo

French athlete Taig Khris is a hero of the inline skating world, but is as well-known by the French public for skating off tall buildings. Having taken a plunge from the first floor of the Eiffel Tower in 2010, Khris now jumped from the Sacré-Coeur – the highest point in Paris. He flew down the 492-foot (150-metre) ramp, taking off with the whole city behind him, and soft-landed on an inflatable half-pipe. He set a new world distance record with a long jump of 95 feet (290 metres).

▼ Daring Descent

https://youtu.be/svfI-bTdMcI

Tianmen Mountain in China is a major tourist attraction, famous for its water-eroded cave and its flight of 999 stairs, but since 2017 it has also been home to the world's longest parkour course, which covers the entirety of the stairs. This video, which went viral and collected over 15 million views, was shot by 19-year-old Calen Chan as he vaulted down the course in just over two minutes. It's fabulously exciting and surprisingly well shot, as Chan didn't have a head or chest strap for his GoPro and filmed the descent with his camera in his mouth.

THE WORLD'S LONGEST PARKOUR COURSE

◄ Russian BASE Jumper

http://y2u.be/oQjp0DgqWpg

Russian extreme-sports star Valery Rozov endured a 31-day expedition to reach the site of his record-breaking BASE jump. In 2013, he had performed the highest-ever BASE jump on Mount Everest, but that wasn't enough for the adrenaline junkie. In 2016, he climbed to just below the summit of the sixth-highest mountain in the world, Cho Oyu in China, in an attempt to better his record. From a height of over 25,000 feet (7,700 metres), Valery leaped off the mountain, spending 90 seconds in free-fall before his parachute opened, and landed on a glacier 5,500 feet (1,700 metres) below and 11,500 feet (3,500 metres) away.

Mountain High

https://youtu.be/NEA0aGcbAVQ

Dani Arnold is a speed climber and in September 2019 he set a world record time for climbing the north face of the Cima Grande, a peak in the Dolomites in northern Italy, via the particularly challenging Comici route. The ascent took him 46 minutes and 30 seconds, but what was even more impressive is that Dani is a free climber, so he doesn't use equipment – no special boots, no ropes, just ordinary trainers and his bare hands. Absolutely terrifying!

▼ Back-Breaking Work

http://y2u.be/Z-OsL4eCgP0

Records don't just happen. New Zealand's Jed Mildon not only spent three intensive months training for his historic triple BMX backflip, but also had to build a super-ramp, 66 feet (20.12 metres) high, into a hillside in order to do it. Jed had kept his attempt to become the first-ever rider to perform three full backwards rotations secret before attempting it in front of 2,000 spectators. They watched spellbound as he careered down the long ramp, shot up a 11.8-foot (3.6-metre) super-kicker, became airborne and created history.

RECORD TRIPLE BACKFLIP

▼ Jet Set

https://youtu.be/y6VlzFj8LBQ

Richard Browning is wearing over-sized binoculars on his arms, a long orange skirt and weird cardboard fins on his ankles. He doesn't exactly look cool, but the jet suit he invented really is. From beside the pier on the beach at Brighton on the UK's south coast, he zooms out over the sea at 85 mph (137 km/h), leaving a trail of sparks behind him. This makes him the holder of the world speed record in a jet suit. Way to go.

**FASTEST
JET-ENGINE
POWER SUIT**

SUPER SPORTS STARS

You don't have to be a big-time pro to be a sporting record breaker. A former NASA scientist, a teenage cheerleader and 6,000 students all wrote their name in the book in style.

FIRST BALLOON KEEP UP WORLD CUP

Hop, Skip, Jump

https://youtu.be/kVHFc1RQ-HQ

This team of precision speed-skippers are Chinese middle school students. There are 12 of them. Ten of them jump very, very quickly, while the other two turn the rope, although that rope is going so fast you can barely see it. The girls link arms, the boys just lean in, but it's ridiculously intense. They are going after the record for the most simultaneous jumps over a single rope in one minute. It's like machine gun fire as they do 225 jumps. That's more than three and a half jumps per second.

▼ Keep it up!

https://youtu.be/liigz06_lvM

Balloon Keep Up is a game that's been played for years, usually at Christmas. You've probably played it yourself, diving across the sofa and trying not to send mum's best vase or the tree flying as you desperately attempt to stop the balloon hitting the ground. And now there's a World Cup event, held on a set that resembles a living room, with a car added for the last stage (of course!). The first tournament took place in Tarragona, Spain, in 2021. Teams from 32 countries participated, with Peru and Germany patting it out in an exciting, first-ever final.

Back in (Fast) Time

https://youtu.be/XVQCkM6X-Aw

Aaron Yoder from Kansas, USA, is going backwards fast. He holds the record for the fastest backward-running mile, stopping the clock at a ridiculous 5 minutes and 54 seconds. After a knee injury stopped a promising forward-running career, Aaron started going backwards and turned to "retro-running". Now a recognized sport with its own World Championships, backwards running puts very little stress on the knee and other joints (although you probably get the odd cricked neck!) In just over three years, Aaron became the fastest backwards human over 200 metres, 1,000 metres and the mile (1.6 km).

Table Service

https://youtu.be/dhzFd-hoGB0

From the late 1990s through to 2007, Eric Finkelstein competed in many national table tennis championships as one of the top junior players in the US. Time moved on and so did Eric, his sporting career coming to an early end. Then, in 2020, he noticed a world record for the longest table tennis serve had been recorded. His competitive spirit reignited, Eric spent months developing and practising his new overhead tennis-style technique, before launching his own attempt on the 48 feet, 9 inch (14.86 metres) record.

▲ Putting It Right

http://y2u.be/htmbMSRj1SQ

Dave Pelz quit being a NASA scientist in 1976 to concentrate on his golf coaching. Using scientific methods, he became an expert in the "short game" – shots made from within around 100 yards (91 metres) of the hole. In 2004, his research paid off. Filming a TV segment for the Golf Channel during PGA Championship week at Whistling Straits in Kohler, Wisconsin, Pelz holed a 206-foot (62.79-metre) putt – beating broadcaster Terry Wogan's previous record of 33 yards (30.2 metres) at Gleneagles.

HIGHEST BASKET EVER MADE

◀ Thunder Strikes Again

http://y2u.be/Wnz4ok5GkZg

Harlem Globetrotters' Thunder Law is the team's designated record-breaker. Longest backwards shot (see page 54), longest basketball shot blindfolded, longest shot while sitting and now highest upwards shot records have all fallen to the 6 feet, 3 inches (1.905-metre) tall player sporting the number 34. His latest entry in the record books came in 2017 in front of the grand staircase at the Utah State Capitol in Salt Lake City. A hoop was hung from a crane at a height of 50 feet and 1 inch (15.27 metres) and the result was surely never in doubt.

PURE STRENGTH

You won't see weights being lifted like this down the local gym. These guys pull, flip and lift in eye-watering feats of strength that just don't seem possible.

Bend an Ear

https://youtu.be/4E2WR_ZpD4w

Daredevil performer Johnny Strange set the record for lifting weights using just chains attached to his ears when he picked up 50 pounds (22.6 kg), the equivalent of a bicycle hanging from each ear, to earn himself the title of "the man with ears of steel" (you can see that on YouTube, too). Now you can't go around with a moniker like that without flaunting it, so here's Johnny again, this time pulling the heaviest weight ever – obviously with his ears – as he lugs a 1500-lb (680 kg) Cessna 172-P aircraft over 66 feet (20 metres).

Hook, Line and Sinker

http://y2u.be/WgGg0innugM

You don't get given the nickname "The Human Toolbox" for nothing. Among his sword-swallowing and bed-of-nails stunts, extreme entertainer Brad Byers is also given to inserting various items – nails, drill bits, hooks – into his head, usually through the nasal cavity. So, here's a warning: if you are squeamish, this video might not be for you. We see Brad insert a hook and pull along a full multi-person bicycle weighing nearly a ton. It's an obscure record but a mighty impressive one: The Heaviest Load Pulled from a Hook in the Head!

EXTREME HOOK INSERTIONS

▼ Steel Yourself

http://y2u.be/k9rQAOp3xVQ

Amandeep Singh is the Indian Man of Steel – a guy who has immense body strength, seemingly feels no pain and is surely as mad as a box of frogs. Witness his show reel, where he makes his bid to be known as the World's Strongest Man. It's difficult not to wince as he retains a grip on ropes holding back 20 motorcyclists, has a car run over his head and a full-sized truck run over his rear, and takes sledgehammer blows to his most sensitive body parts. Now that's gotta hurt!

A Smashing Time

http://y2u.be/LqisPXXqpEY

What do you do with those pumpkins once Halloween is over? It isn't a problem for Conor Murphy and his trusty tool. Watch him take a sledge hammer to a truckload of pumpkins; there is something immensely satisfying in such wanton destruction. The CrossFit coach from Boston, USA, makes swift work of pumpkin obliteration as he pounds his way through a record 30 orange gourds in just one minute. It's no mean feat. The guy is seriously fit and he not only secured the world record, but doubled the previous total. Now, who's for pumpkin soup?

▼ The Weight of the World

https://youtu.be/2kEC7X1FUIg

Many will know him from the *Game of Thrones* TV series where he plays "The Mountain", but Hafthor Julius Bjornsson is a true life powerhouse. In 2018 he won the title of World's Strongest Man, then in 2020 he became the first man ever to lift more than half a ton. His astonishing lift of 501 kg (approx. 1,000 lbs)– about the weight of a grand piano or a grizzly bear – took place in his own gym due to the coronavirus pandemic. It was just a kilo more than the existing record. "I could have done more," Bjornsson claimed," but what's the point?"

▼ Quick Pit Fitters

https://youtu.be/Bl75uWxEajA

In Formula 1 motor racing a thousandth of a second can be the difference between success and failure. So when driver Max Verstappen pulled in for a tyre change at the 2019 Brazilian Grand Prix his Red Bull team had to be on their toes. In the pit, 16 people stand ready, including four tyre swappers with super-powerful pneumatic wheel guns. Pit stops generally take around 2.4 seconds, but this change took a record 1.82 seconds. This video lasts a whole minute but shows the synchronicity and great teamwork in slow motion and from every angle.

FASTEST
FORMuLA 1
TYRE CHANGE

BACKWARDS RECORDS

Doing something backwards is a favourite among record breakers. Sometimes skilful, sometimes dangerous and often looking rather silly, our heroes set to their task without fear of neck ache ...

◀ Thunder's Back

http://y2u.be/o4fzSkAgNP4

Although it has since been broken, Thunder Law of the Harlem Globetrotters used to hold the record for the longest-ever basketball shot. And although he has had to give up that crown, he can take solace in an even more incredible achievement: the longest shot facing away from the hoop. His one-handed backward launch propelled the ball 82 feet and 2 inches (25 metres) – almost the length of the court and 10 feet (3 metres) further than the previous record – for a perfect three-pointer.

◢ Parallel Parking

http://y2u.be/VSp1olKp_f0

Try this manoeuvre when you're faced with a tight parking space at the local supermarket car park. In front of a live audience at the 2015 Performance Car Show, British stunt driver Alastair Moffatt slid a Fiat 500 1.2 Cult into the narrowest of parallel-parking spaces. Moffat's magnificent handbrake turn was made in a standard car with an enhanced steering wheel and pumped-up tyre pressures. Sliding into a space just 3 inches (7.5 centimetres) longer than the car enabled Moffat to reclaim a world record that had been taken from him by a Chinese stunt driver. He bested his rival by 0.2 inches (5 mm).

Get Your Skates On

https://youtu.be/hWGn_v8uO5E

High heels are usually associated with grace and style, but in truth Canadian circus performer Bianca Rossini is not exactly the picture of perfect elegance as she attempts to set a world record for the fastest 328 feet (100 metres) skating backwards in stilettos. That said, her in-line skates with pink spiky shoes attached do look rather glamorous. Still, the main point here is whether she can stay upright and cross the line in under 30 seconds or fall and fail...

▼ Ramping It Up

http://y2u.be/XUIiffRMfVQ

Ever wondered what skateboarders do for thrills when they grow out of their baggy shorts and elbow pads? Professional skateboarder Rob Dyrdek set 21 different skateboarding records before moving on to be a TV star and all-round entertainer. He broke doughnut-and-banana-eating records on his hit show *Rob & Big*, but once a ramp man ... In the parking lot of a theme park, Dyrdek reversed his Chevrolet Sonic off one ramp and flew 89 feet 3¼ inches (27.2 metres) through the air to land cleanly on another. What a guy!

THE WORLD'S LONGEST REVERSE RAMP JUMP

▶ Bowling Backwards

http://y2u.be/ex5iwpBHhdw

YouTube has opened up an opportunity for records to be broken all over the world. You no longer need officials and men in blazers to set an authentic record, just a clear video of your achievement. Step forward the most unlikely looking hero in Andrew Cowen of Illinois, USA. Andrew was determined to throw a 300 score (pretty impossible for us weekend bowlers) – while facing the wrong way. He managed 280 – two more than the official record – and might have reached his 300 if not for that second frame slip-up.

TOTALLY GROSS!

Are you ready to be completely grossed-out? These are some of the yuckiest, flesh-creeping and nauseating clips on the site. And, of course, they are absolutely mesmerizing.

Mayo-nazing

https://youtu.be/_INKqoqDYsk

Michelle Lesco is a competitive eater. She has consumed plates of pasta and hot dogs at top speed, but she may have met her match in mayonnaise. The challenge is to spoon as much of it as possible into your mouth in three minutes. Somehow she downs three large jars and is well on her way through the fourth when the whistle blows. The record stands at 1.8 pounds (815.5 grams), but Michelle manages to slurp down 5.4 pounds (2448 grams) of the creamy gloop – and seems completely unaffected.

MILK-SQUIRTING CHAMPION

▶ Squirt Off

http://y2u.be/H7EPl1N_aN4

It's the ultimate squirting-milk-from-the-eye battle! Please don't try this at home. It hurts and can lead to lasting damage to the eyes. Plus, it's altogether a pretty repulsive thing to do. That said, have a look at these two heroes squirting it out for the record. The trick, apparently, is to snort milk up your nose, close your mouth, block your nostrils and build up the pressure in the nose. The milk has nowhere else to go but to escape through a duct in the eyes. Yuk!

▼ Cockroach Challenge

http://y2u.be/jtXXWz-iKKQ

Even if celebrity reality-TV shows have made you rather blasé about the eating of creepy crawlies, this record by Travis Fessler of Florence, Kentucky, still leaves an uneasy taste in the mouth. Fessler takes on the world record for putting the most Madagascar Hissing Cockroaches in his mouth. It's enough that he can bear to pick up one of the critters let alone have room to stuff 11 roaches into his mouth at the same time. Animal lovers can relax: all 11 reappear, looking healthy and as disgusting as ever.

MOST COCKROACHES HELD IN THE MOUTH

▼ Prized Poo!

https://youtu.be/cBEmZs5Z7Zs

In a glass box at the Jorvik Viking Centre in York sits a fascinating item. It is an eight-inch (20.3-centimetres) long and two-inch (5-centimetres) wide coprolite – the official term for fossilised poo. This is the largest single piece of human excrement ever discovered. The Lloyds Bank coprolite (it was found under a branch of the bank) dates back to the 9th century and is believed to have been expelled by a Viking man. Paleoscatologists studying the ancient log have ascertained that he ate mostly meat and bread, and was suffering from stomach problems!

MULTIPLE RECORD HOLDERS

For some people, breaking one mention in the record books is just not enough. One sniff of glory has them searching for more.

JOE ALEXANDER

MOST MARSHMALLOWS CAUGHT WITH CHOPSTICKS

It's a Wrap

https://youtu.be/HZIKyEG8TFk

Don't worry, if you're trying to take the record for the fastest time to wrap someone in cling film or saran wrap, the person you're wrapping will still be able to breathe, because fortunately you only have to cover them from the neck down. David Rush, who loves breaking obscure records, has his wife step in to be his mannequin. Admittedly, she doesn't look that happy about it, and although it does take him 12 attempts and around 1,000 feet (over 300 metres) of plastic, he gets it in the end – to Mrs Rush's great relief!

◀ Joe of all Trades

http://y2u.be/vilul1gCm64

Joe Alexander from Hamburg, Germany, likes a record or two. Well, 10 at the last count. Joe doesn't seem fussy as long as they are records. Among his successes are smashing concrete tiles while holding an egg in his hand, catching marshmallows with chopsticks, and trapping harpoons underwater. On record-breaking day 2013, the self-styled Adrenalin Master gave us two records for the price of one. First up, he walked across 60 champagne bottles in a row without touching the ground. He then followed that up by catching 16 darts with his bare hands.

POP'S MOST SUCCESSFUL MUSICIAN

◢Off the Charts

https://youtu.be/vNQIDsDWJZM

You can't keep BTS, the global kings of K-pop, out of the record books. In September 2021 they held 21 world records, including being the most streamed group on Spotify, the most followed band on Instagram and the group with the most Twitter engagements. Their 2021 hit 'Butter' won them a heap more. It had the biggest YouTube premiere in history with 3.9 million concurrent viewers, and when it returned to No.1 in the Billboard charts, replacing their own 'Permission to Dance' (which had knocked it off the spot), they became the first-ever act to replace themselves at number one – twice!

▲ Houston, We Have a ... Beatle

http://y2u.be/hpvE8kVGeZI

Once a member of the Beatles, Paul McCartney has gone on to become the most successful musician and composer in popular music history. He has a host of sales and radio-play world records, the most Number 1 hits ever, the most frequently covered song in history ("Yesterday" has been sung by over 4,000 artists), the largest paid audience for a solo concert (350,000 people, in 1989 in Brazil) – and, perhaps best of all, he was the first artist to broadcast live to space.

BRILLIANT BUILDINGS

Yes, it's interesting to discover the dates and dimensions of the world's record-breaking buildings, but how much better is it to watch one tilting sideways, or being climbed without ropes?

Head for Heights

http://y2u.be/a2p4BOGXSBw

Do you suffer from vertigo? If so, maybe give this video a miss. Here, a man known only as "Urban Endeavors" takes us up 1,500 feet (475 metres), twice the height of the Eiffel Tower, to the very top of the world's tallest TV tower, in North Dakota, USA. The tower itself is an unexceptional structure, but the journey is nail-biting and breathtaking as our guide climbs without ropes or harness; just gloves and bucketfuls of courage. He even forgoes the "easy way up", climbing the outside of the tower, rather than using the central ladder.

▶ Demolition Dhabi

https://youtu.be/WfTkzbTt8qY

In November 2020, the skyline of Abu Dhabi in the United Arab Emirates changed in the space of ten seconds. The four Mina Plaza Towers, with a combined total of 144 floors, had stood for just over a decade and, though still unfinished, had become a landmark in the city. However, new development plans for the port led to the 540-foot (165-metre) towers becoming the world's tallest buildings to be demolished using explosives. To bring them down, 5.9 tons (6 tonnes) of explosives were placed in 18,000 holes drilled around the structure. The blast from the controlled implosion was heard across the capital.

DOWN IN TEN SECONDS

▶ A Tilt at the Record

http://y2u.be/UEfeqgXPHPA

Everyone has heard of the Leaning Tower of Pisa, some have heard of the leaning tower of Suurhusen (which leans a further 1.22 degrees). However, as of 2010, there is a new leaning king on the block – the Capital Gate in Abu Dhabi. In contrast to the previous record holders, the Capital Gate was intentionally designed to lean. Despite being one of the tallest buildings in the city at 35 storeys high, it keels as much as 18° westwards – more than four times that of Suurhusen.

▶ Go with the Flow

https://youtu.be/xzDs462Gtz0

The first time it was turned on, local residents called the local paper, because they thought the pipes had burst. In fact, the running costs are so high that it isn't turned on very often and then only for 20 minutes at a time. However, the world's tallest man-made waterfall in action is a quite a sight to behold. The water cascades 354 feet (108 metres) down one face of the Liebian International Building, a 397-foot (121-metre) skyscraper in Guiyang, in southern China's Guizhou Province.

TALLEST MAN-MADE WATERFALL

King of the Castles

https://youtu.be/BrXcwzbdnGo

While many people will want to forget about the coronavirus pandemic as quickly as possible, Dutch artist Wilfred Stijger decided to make a monument to it – in sand. Using 4,860 tonnes of sand reinforced with glue and clay, he built a pyramid-style structure in the Danish seaside town of Blokhus. Decorated with mini-sculptures of local sights, it was topped with a model of the coronavirus wearing a crown. Looking down from a height of 69.4 feet (21.16 metres) – the world's tallest ever sandcastle – it represented the power the pandemic had exerted on the whole world.

▼ Reflected Glory

https://youtu.be/AuzezyqlvYM

Heading through the desert of the Al-Ula region of Saudi Arabia you'd be forgiven for thinking that the huge mirrored building in front of you is a mirage. But this incredible shiny construction, which reflects the ever-changing desert, carved rocks and cave art of the neighbourhood, is very real. In fact, it's the Maraya Concert Hall, a 105,000 square foot (9,700 square metre) building in the region's Unesco World Heritage site. "Maraya", meaning "mirror" in Arabic, is covered with reflective panels, making it the largest mirrored building in the world.

WORLD'S MOST MIRRORED BUILDING

SUPER-FAST RECORDS

The best records are those feats we think we can do pretty well ourselves. Just watch these people get dressed, cut hair or throw a Frisbee – and see if you might match them.

Cold Feet

https://youtu.be/-FWFL_6NVd0

Here we have David Rush (he is obsessed with breaking records and you might remember him from page 58) attempting the record for the most socks removed in one minute while blindfolded. Now, there are a number of ways you could do this, but David's set-up is quite simple. It consists of a long line of chairs. There's someone sitting in each chair and… well, you'll see. The terms of the record don't state whether the socks have to be clean or not, but let's hope so.

In the Balance

http://y2u.be/bDFZok9uzdk

Try to balance an egg. It isn't easy, they are just not made for it. It would take most people five minutes to balance one egg. Back in 2003, Brian Spotts helped break the record of most eggs balanced at once with 1,290 eggs. But he was hungry for more records, so he invented the category of fastest time to balance a dozen eggs. Finding his record broken, Brian decided it was time to poach it back – at a shopping mall in Hong Kong.

▼ Plot Twist

http://y2u.be/5x8jgGX3iNM

The Rubik's Cube was invented in 1974 (by Ernő Rubik, of course!) and first went on sale in 1980. With around 350 million cubes sold to date, it is the world's best-selling puzzle game. And a constant world-record challenge. Step forward SeungBeom Cho, the most recent record-breaker. He set his incredible 4.59-second record for the 3 x 3 x 3 cube in a competition in Chicago, USA, in 2017. Now, 23-year-old Cho is a highly rated speed-cuber, but his surprise at taking the record is absolutely priceless.

FASTEST RUBIK'S CUBE SOLVER

▶ A Cut Above

http://y2u.be/C1k1kiAd3Bg

There was no time for niceties. No enquiry about holiday destinations. Not even a question about "how would you like your hair today, sir?" Hairdresser Konstantinos Koutoupis from Athens, Greece, had no time to waste if he was going to secure the record for giving the fastest haircut. The rules stated it had to be a "businessman haircut", taking at least half an inch (1.5 centimetres) off all round the head, so Konstantinos couldn't cut corners. With his mirrors cleaned, scissors sharpened and the customer's hair finely combed, Konstantinos had just 50 seconds to deliver…

▼ Sling Shot

http://y2u.be/NRr2zL0PYPA

You wouldn't want to get in the way of a 100-mph (160-km/h) ball thrown by an MLB baseball pitcher or, indeed, face a test cricketer bowling at you at 90 mph (145 km/h). It is, however, Jai Alai – popular in the Basque region, Latin America and the Philippines – that is recognised as the fastest sport in the world. Played on a 175-foot (53-metre) long court with three walls by teams of two players, each with curved baskets that are strapped to their hands, the game sees players consistently catch and throw balls at an incredible 186 mph (300 k/ph).

Speedy Frisbee

http://y2u.be/TO2RQj-L7gg

Simon Lizotte was a Frisbee prodigy. Dubbed "The Wunderkind", Lizotte, from Bremen in Germany, has dominated the German Disc Golf scene for years. He was the 2012 European Champion and is renowned in the game for his power on the drive. He holds the record for the longest disc throw (863.5 feet or 263.2 metres – the length of two-and-a-half football pitches), but here he notches up the fastest throw ever recorded at 89.5 mph (144 km/h).

WORLD'S FASTEST SPORT

SOUND AND VISION

They say it takes all sorts to make a world ... but the record world has the strangest inhabitants of all. Call them weird, call them mad; they call themselves "record breakers"!

Rock Bottom

https://youtu.be/FgP6ij1H-FY

When you think of underground music you probably have an indie band or a rap artist in mind, not four middle-aged guys playing good-time rock and roll. Then again, maybe the Shaft Bottom Boys are more subterranean than underground, because in 2020 they performed a 50-minute set at the foot of the Vale's Creighton Mine in Sudbury, Ontario, 6,213 feet (1,894 metres) below sea level. Fitted out, for safety reasons, in regulation orange work overalls and hard hats, and playing to a similarly dressed crowd, they rocked the underworld in the deepest ever gig.

CONCERT BY AN UNDERGROUND SENSATION

▶ Fan-tastic Noise

https://youtu.be/JwUuU1M5y_U

Sports fans around the world frequently boast that their team has the loudest support. However, supporters of Kansas University's basketball team, the Jayhawks, can support their claim with an official record. In February 2017, at their Allen Fieldhouse arena, after a game against West Virginia, screaming fans reached a world record level for an indoor crowd of 130.4 decibels. Just to put it in context, live rock music is around 110dB and a chainsaw can reach 120dB. Now that's what you call getting behind your team. Go, Jayhawks!

Ace of Bass

https://youtu.be/NoChroQIA10

Italian Davide Biale is better known as "YouTuber Davie504". His fans, and there are an awful lot of them, are known as "slappers" – a reference to the bass guitar-playing technique called slapping – and his often-repeated catchphrase is "Slap like now!" In case it's not obvious, Davie is obsessed with the bass. So obsessed that he's built the world's only 36-string bass. It's a strange-looking instrument and clearly quite tricky to handle, but he really can play and he treats us to a virtuoso performance.

OLDEST PERSON TO RELEASE AN ALBUM

▲ Lifetime Achievement

https://youtu.be/xyTa_gJkYwI

Singer Tony Bennett fought in World War II, had his first number one record in 1951 and went on to sell 500 million records worldwide. Throughout his career he has reached out to new generations and, despite being diagnosed with Alzheimer's in 2016, continued to seek new audiences. At the age of 95 years and 60 days, he became the oldest person to release an album of new material with *Love For Sale*, a collaboration with Lady Gaga that also earned him the record for the longest span of top-ten albums for any living artist (his first top-ten hit was 'I Left My Heart in San Francisco' in 1962).

CRAZY CRITTERS

There's no such thing as a fair fight in the wild. Clawing, biting, stinging and kicking are all allowed. These guys are the best in the business.

Angry Bird

http://y2u.be/mb1bbIyF9OU

Hailing from the rain forests of Australia and New Guinea, the cassowary has a bony crest on its head capable of knocking down small trees, and dagger-like sharp claws. Growing up to 6 feet (1.82 metres) tall and weighing in at over 130 pounds (59 kilograms), it can reach speeds of 30 mph (48 km/h) – and is capable of kicking with both legs at the same time. They have gutted dogs, slaughtered horses and maimed and even killed humans. The most dangerous bird by far …

Sting in the Tail

http://y2u.be/cWl66-HBnOM

Say hello to the *Androctonus australis* – but don't get too close. The creature's name means "southern man-killer" and, indeed, the fat-tailed scorpion, as it is commonly known, is the deadliest scorpion in the world. Found in the deserts of the Middle East and Africa, the venom of the fat-tailed scorpion causes several human deaths every year. The killer critters aren't huge – they only grow up to 4 inches (10 centimetres) long – but are often found hiding in the brickwork or concrete cracks of houses. So go careful where you put those fingers!

▶ Packing a Punch

http://y2u.be/ti2Uoc1RXuQ

The mantis shrimp is a fabulous creature. A shrimp-sized lobster, it has big bug eyes, comes in dazzling colours and packs the fastest and strongest punch in the animal kingdom. Sometimes referred to as "thumb splitters", their claws are strong enough to split human appendages, and the shrimp has a punch stronger than a .22-calibre pistol. It has even been known to smash the glass of aquariums when riled. Just watch this slow-motion footage of this champion slugger throwing a right hook!

THE SHRIMP THAT PACKS A PUNCH

▶ Iron Jaws

http://y2u.be/akbpHX0Wbvw

The human bite exerts a pressure of around 120 psi (pounds per square inch). It's enough to chomp through an apple or a piece of toffee. Lions and sharks have jaws that are five times as strong – good for tearing raw flesh apart or ripping through a small boat. But the iron jaws of the animal world belong to the Nile crocodile. These beasts can snap at 2,500 psi (and have reached 6,000 psi), twice as much again as the feared shark.

▼ Make it Snappy

https://youtu.be/H2okI6ZszQY

Welcome to the Ant Lab. The trap-jaw ant, known in Latin as *Andontomachus brunneus*, has a super-fast and super-powerful spring-lever jaw. When it attacks, its lower jaw moves at a mind-bending 90 mph (145 km/h), which is roughly the speed of a bullet in the barrel of a gun. One open-and-shut bite takes 312 micro-seconds or one three-thousandth of a second to complete. Just capturing this action in super-slow-motion video is no mean feat, involving both physics and maths. However the question here is, in the battle of the ant versus a finger, who will win?

THE WORLD'S QUICKEST BITE

AMAZING FOOD RECORDS

Groceries – they're not just for eating, you know. You can use them in art, construction, as a pastime – and to break records. Here's some food for thought ...

▼ Pumpkin Pride

http://y2u.be/8eQljtg3tAA

This was the moment the pumpkin world had been waiting for: the first-ever one-tonne pumpkin, winning farmer Ron Wallace a $10,000 prize. The historical event happened in 2012 at the All New England Giant Pumpkin Weigh-Off when Wallace's colossal pumpkin was lifted onto the scale by a forklift truck. It topped out at an astounding 2,009 pounds (911 kilograms), beating the record set just the previous day by 165 pounds (75 kilograms) to become the largest fruit ever grown.

Hand to Mouth

https://youtu.be/ZelypGV9uuw

David Rush is a prolific record breaker (you'll find his feats elsewhere in this book) and he will try pretty much anything to help promote STEM education. Here he takes on the record for most marshmallows caught in the mouth in one minute. In fact, this is a feat you might fancy trying for yourself. First, study Dave's technique and then the role played by Jonathan 'Hollywood' Hanlon, his marshmallow-throwing partner. A steady hand and dead-eye aim are just as important as the agile and gaping mouth that captures them, especially if you're going to catch a marshmallow every second, which is what you need to do to come close to breaking this record.

THE INCREDIBLE ONE-TON PUMPKIN

70

FUNKY FUNKO MOSAIC

◀ Most Massive Modhesh

https://youtu.be/WtZS9XHIP4Q

For nearly 20 years, a chirpy, yellow, worm-like figure has popped up on street corners and in shops across the United Arab Emirates to promote the Dubai Summer Surprises festival. Its name is Modhesh (pronounced Mud-hish) and it appears on thousands of items, from novelty pens to cuddly toys. In 2020, Modhesh – whose name means "excited" – was honoured by plastic figure manufacturer Funko with a huge mosaic. At Dubai's world-famous Mall of the Emirates it took 16 hours to put together the largest packaged product mosaic in the world. It used 8,600 plastic figures and measured 1,700 square feet (158 square metres).

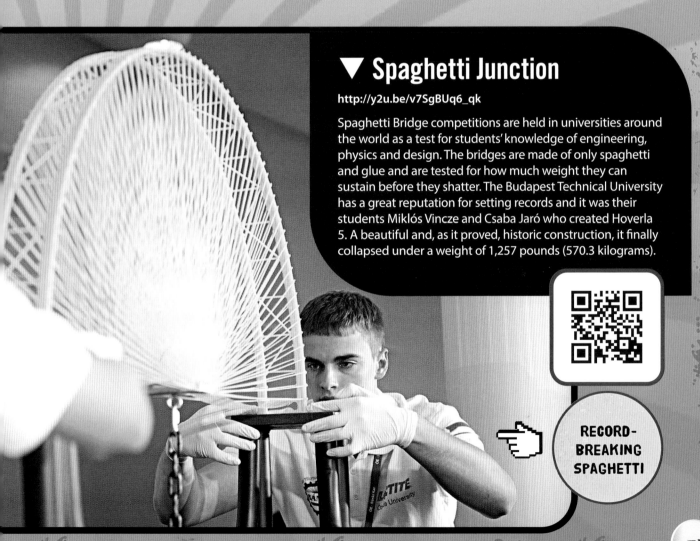

▼ Spaghetti Junction

http://y2u.be/v7SgBUq6_qk

Spaghetti Bridge competitions are held in universities around the world as a test for students' knowledge of engineering, physics and design. The bridges are made of only spaghetti and glue and are tested for how much weight they can sustain before they shatter. The Budapest Technical University has a great reputation for setting records and it was their students Miklós Vincze and Csaba Jaró who created Hoverla 5. A beautiful and, as it proved, historic construction, it finally collapsed under a weight of 1,257 pounds (570.3 kilograms).

RECORD-BREAKING SPAGHETTI

SUPER-STRENGTH RECORDS

The human body is a wonderful thing and even if you think you've seen it all, there's always something weird out there that will blow your mind: these record-breakers, for example.

On the Nail

http://y2u.be/W13JvvsKiJM

Extreme-stunts performer "Space Cowboy" calls himself "Australia's most prolific record breaker" – and with good reason. He has over 40 records to his name (which is really Chayne Hultgren), including pulling 906 pounds (411 kg) by fishhooks in his eye sockets for the furthest distance, the fastest arrow caught blindfolded, and most chainsaw-juggling catches on a unicycle. In 2012, the Cowboy displayed his skills on the TV Show *Australia's Got Talent*. Lying on a bed of over 100 sharp, 8-inch (20-centimetre) nails, he was driven over by 20 motorcycles in 2 minutes.

◄ Busting his Nuts

http://y2u.be/OD1g8fUFdxQ

If you're struggling with the nutcracker again this Christmas, you could try breaking those shells manually. All you need is a little iron-palm training. That's how this martial-arts master gained the strength to set a new world record in Foshan City in southern China's Guangdong Province in 2017. He smashed 302 walnuts in 55 seconds with his bare hands. Before you give it a go, though, bear in mind that kung-fu expert Li Weijun has trained in various kinds of Chinese martial arts for over 27 years.

MONSTER WALNUT-CRUSHER

▶ Dinnie Time

https://youtu.be/xawxgX9OGOk

The Dinnie Stones are a pair of giant uneven boulders located in Potarch, Aberdeenshire. They are made of granite and have a combined weight of 733.1 pounds (332 kilos). Despite the attached iron rings, lifting them is all but impossible for most, and only a handful of people have succeeded in lifting them without straps. Holding them or carrying them 'farmer's style' has become a challenge for the world's leading strongmen. In August 2021, one of the most renowned of modern strongmen, Laurence "Big Loz" Shahlaei, travelled to Scotland to attempt to write his name in the history of this legendary challenge.

Thigh High

http://y2u.be/TN59gYxa2to

The sport of crushing fruit between your thighs isn't likely to threaten the popularity of football on TV any time soon, but Olga Liaschuk's appearance on British TV show *This Morning* caused quite a stir. Seated on a mat in the studio, and watched over by genial show hosts Phillip Schofield and Holly Willoughby, Olga crushed 3 watermelons between her thighs in just 14 seconds. Ukrainian Olga is also a champion in the perfectly respectable sport of weightlifting, but who wants to watch that when you can see exploding melons?

▼ Miracle Man

https://youtu.be/b-tFgKlqgb0

Mark Felix is 53 years old or, as he prefers to put it, 53 years young, and he's a plasterer by day, strongman by night. He only started entering strongman competitions at 38, but since then he's made up for lost time and qualified for the World's Strongest Man event 14 times. No wonder he's known as "The Miracle". Mark trains hard, but also has a handspan of 11 inches (28 cm). This probably helps when it comes to the Hercules hold world record, which involves preventing two steel pillars, each weighing 772 pounds (350 kg), from toppling over…

Table Manners

http://y2u.be/MC6tgknKPQE

Even among strongmen challenges, some records push the boundaries of the bizarre. Take Georges Christen, a national hero in Luxembourg. In a career spanning over 30 years, Georges has made a name for himself setting records pulling trucks, buses and ships, and even making a huge Ferris wheel turn – all using his teeth. This performance – a repeat of another record-breaking feat – is a little more special. It shows a woman sitting on a table being carried in the air by Georges – yep, you've guessed it – by his teeth! She's seems like a willing participant, but keep an eye on her expression.

HOLDING OUT FOR A HERO

This awesome selection illustrates just how wide-ranging the record-breaking heroes are. Some rely on physical endurance, others on know-how and some are just downright crazy!

◀ Room on the Back

http://y2u.be/6qRzC95YpSE

Plumber Colin Furze's project began in his mum's garden with a normal 125cc scooter, which the ingenious engineer adapted with a home-made aluminium frame, adding 25 seats and extending it to 72 feet (22 metres) – nearly as long as a tennis court. To set the record, Furze had to ride the bike for 328 feet (100 metres), but he actually rode it for over a mile (1.6 kilometres). "When I first got on it, I thought it would never work, and at a slow speed it's almost impossible to keep upright," says Colin, but on Saltby Airfield in Grantham, England, he managed a pretty impressive 35 mph (56 km/h).

MOST DRUMBEATS IN A MINUTE

▶ Drumroll Please!

https://youtu.be/JrnPBnRegUU?t=568

At the age of two and a half, Siddharth Nagarajan played his first concert and was officially recognized as the youngest ever Indian drummer. Six years later, having been invited onto a National Geographic TV show, he was declared an inborn genius. Now, at the age of 19, Siddharth is a respected percussionist across musical genres and a world-record holder. In 2017, he broke the record for The Most Drumbeats in a Minute Using Drumsticks. His 2,109 beats is equivalent to a staggering 35 beats in a second. Now that's how you "beat" a record.

▼ Fast Track

http://y2u.be/H7IwEQGM_Vk

There are many records in this book that are foolish, dangerous or outright idiotic, but this is the only one that is actually criminal. The clip tells the story of Ed Bolian's attempt at the Cannonball Baker Sea to Shining Sea Memorial Trophy Dash, a coast-to-coast drive across the USA and the basis for the movie *The Cannonball Run*. It's a highly illegal race that requires speed limits to be broken all through the journey. Ed reached a top speed of 158.26 mph (255 km/h) and spent 88 per cent of the trip above 80 mph (128 km/h), but he did traverse the country in just 28 hours and 50 minutes.

THE FASTEST DRIVE ACROSS THE USA

Swiss Roll

https://youtu.be/Tez12O9zKZU

The video calls it Swiss ball surfing, but there is no beach and no waves – just a running track and a line of those air-filled exercise (Swiss or Ballast) balls you see in the gym. Aussie Nicholas Smith lines up 26 of these giant balls and precedes to "surf" along the line from one to another, covering a record distance of 255 feet, 4.96 inches (77.85 metres). Some may dispute the "surfing" aspect and say that "belly-bouncing" would be a more accurate description, but there can be no denying that it looks like a whole lot of fun.

FURTHEST SWISS BALL "SURF"

Underwater Workout

https://youtu.be/b1hqcWpAIAA

Vitaly Vivchar from Tomsk in Siberia had not only won the European Russian-style bench press tournament, he was also an amateur free diver, so when he saw there was a record for performing bench presses underwater it seemed like it already had his name written on it. He trained for two months before attempting the record at Lebyazhye Lake in Russia. The weight was nothing special – just 110 pounds (50 kilograms) – but he's holding his breath while submerged in cold, muddy water and still managing to smash out 76 reps. Respect.

TOTALLY DIFFERENT

The record breaker can never stop to ask why. Thankfully, these record setters never questioned putting themselves in harm's way, playing a silly instrument or throwing shaving-foam pies …

Egg-ceptional Strength

https://youtu.be/S3Q1Zio7IMw

Martial arts practitioner Muhammad Rashid from Pakistan already held some bizarre records, such as most bottle caps removed with the head in one minute and most green coconuts smashed with the head in one minute. That didn't stop him taking on the challenge of most unopened drinks cans crushed by hand in 30 seconds while holding an egg. It was a daunting task that required strength, accuracy and the sensitivity not to smash the egg as he brought his hand down on the can. Could Muhammad smash it or would the yoke be on him?

WORLD'S LARGEST CROCHET BLANKET

▼ Splat's the way to do it!

http://y2u.be/sKOqUJfcUfw

And you think flinging foam pies is just clowns playing around? Listen, there are rules to this sport. The plates must be filled with shaving foam, which has to have a peak, and the flinger must be 5 feet (1.5 metres) away from the victim. And so to the Kidtropolis show in London in 2017, where "Captain Calamity" and "Colonel Custard" (probably not their real names) are on their fourth attempt at the record for the most shaving-foam pies flung in someone's face in one minute. They have already equalled the record but, if they are going to better it, they need to keep their eyes on the pies…

MOST "PIES" THROWN IN FACE

◀ Raw Geometry

http://y2u.be/C7XY-HvNWas

In the summer of 2016, sushi mosaics were trending on Instagram. Hundreds of pictures showed sushi squares, artistically arranged in colourful geometric patterns. It is a quintessentially Japanese art form – they are exquisite, delicate and precise – so, naturally, the world record for the largest sushi mosaic was set in… Norway, and was created by a chef who runs a sushi bar in Sweden. The mosaic, displayed at the Aspmyra Stadion, in Bode, Norway, measured an incredible 608 square feet (56.50 square metres) and included almost 1,800 pounds (800 kilograms) of salmon, around 900 pounds (400 kilograms) of rice, 44 gallons (200 litres) of rice vinegar, 1,060 pounds (480 kilograms) of cucumber and 22 pounds (10 kilograms) of chives.

WORLD'S LARGEST SuSHI MOSAIC

▼ What a Reaction

https://youtu.be/XXn4fP3CnJg

Elephant's toothpaste is the name given to foam that you can make by mixing the chemical hydrogen peroxide, warm water and a catalyst like yeast or, in this case, potassium iodide. Nick Uhas and the V.Squad have a history of conducting this experiment on a grand scale and here they go for the world record. There's a lot of preparation, some neat DIY and some interesting science involved – and the results are truly spectacular. However, for a number of reasons (see what happens to fellow YouTuber David Dobrik's Los Angeles house) remember not to try this at home!

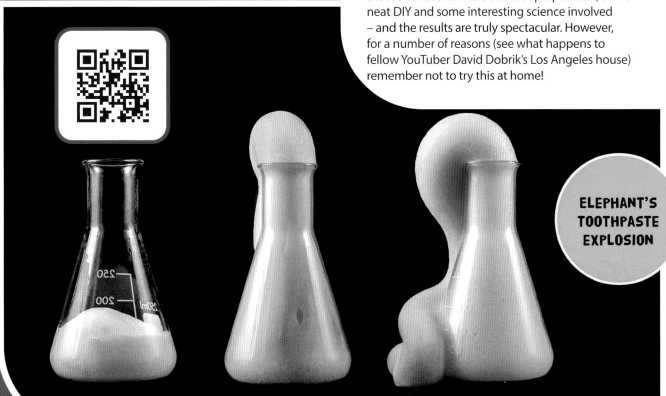

ELEPHANT'S TOOTHPASTE EXPLOSION

COOL CAT RECORDS

There is plenty of kitten action and a lot of celebrity cats on YouTube, but not many make the record books. Here's a select few who are on the road to purr-fection.

Top Cat

https://youtu.be/zjhBrlE-tBw

Meet Nala. She's a Siamese/tabby cross and she's the Kim Kardashian of cats. She holds the world record for the most Instagram followers – 4.3 million and rising – and is officially the most famous cat on the Internet (Grumpy Cat, the previous record-holder, sadly passed away in 2019). Nala is undeniably extremely cute and earns a very good living as an influencer. Her owners are reluctant to reveal exactly how much she makes a year, but it's enough to have bought them not just one, but two, houses.

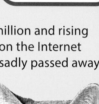

Toe Business

https://youtu.be/7w86n5pmO1Q

While most cats have 18 toes – five on their front paws and four on their back ones – polydactyl cats have extra digits. Polydactyly is an abnormality that is passed from generation to generation. It has no ill effects, in fact their big paws often make them look extra cute and they have super climbing and hunting skills. So meet Paws, a Minnesota cat who ties for a record number of toes. She has 28 toes, three extra on each forepaw and one extra on each back paw. All together now… Awwww!

▶ Cool Cat

http://y2u.be/eCG-wInJJK0

Cats are well known for having great balance. It's pretty useful for traversing garden fences or catching birds. Boomer, however, is far too cool for that kind of nonsense. The Bengali cat hangs out in Australia and likes nothing better than riding his skateboard. Here is Boomer, in October 2017, breaking his own record (13 people) for the longest human tunnel travelled through by a skateboarding cat. He propels himself through 20 pairs of legs – and still acts like it's really no big deal. He's obviously saving the high fives for his first 360 flip.

MOST TALENTED SKATE-BOARDING CAT

▶ Kitten Kong

https://youtu.be/dYUrxlNEgqs

Kittens are adored the world over for being cute and fluffy, with adorable tiny features. Twenty-two-month-old Kefir is just as well-loved, but he's not what you'd call cute. The Maine Coon kitten lives in the Russian town of Stary Oskol, and is so large he's often mistaken for a dog. His owner is keen to stress that Kefir is just as playful, affectionate and lovable as any mini-moggie, but the white-furred puss already weighs more than most adult Maine Coons, registering a hefty 27 pounds (12.5 kg) on the scales. That makes him the world's largest kitten, and he still has two years or more growing to do.

WORLD'S LARGEST KITTEN

◢ Big Big Cat

http://y2u.be/cNJVI0e6Zhw

There are cats, big cats and then there are ligers. Ligers are the offspring of a male lion and a tigress – huge animals that do not exist in the wild and are only bred in captivity. Hercules, who usually lives at the Myrtle Beach Safari wildlife preserve in South Carolina, is the biggest of them all. He is 6 feet (1.82 metres) tall, 12 feet (3.65 metres) long and weighs 900 pounds (408 kilograms) – as big as his parents combined. He may look a handful, but his keepers say he's a real pussycat.

THE WORLD'S LARGEST LIGER

CRAZY CROWD RECORDS

Whoever said "Three's a crowd" wasn't in the record-breaking business. To register in the record books, you need great organization, silly costumes and people in their thousands ...

▼ Who You Gonna Call?

http://y2u.be/dqQCj7WKNgk

"Ghostbusters of the world, gear up!" went the call to arms from Paul Feig, director of the 2016 version of the 1984 supernatural horror-comedy classic. The fans responded and 263 people got their ghost on – dressed up as the film's famous "no-ghost" logo – and gathered at Singapore's Marina Bay Sands to celebrate the launch of the all-female reboot of the *Ghostbusters* film. Star of the movie Melissa McCarthy was also in attendance and in high spirits as the assembly claimed the title of "Largest gathering of people dressed as ghosts at a single venue".

WORLD'S LARGEST GHOST GATHERING

Follow the Leader

http://y2u.be/yg17h5H9YUM

The record for the most people singing in a round was previously held by the Dublin Google office, where 3,798 employees sang Pharell Williams'"Happy". The new record could not be more different, as to achieve it a choir of 4,166 people in Turkmenistan sang a song penned by the president. The performance of "Forward Only Forward, My Dear Country Turkmenistan" featured a big-screen video of President Berdimuhamedow himself playing a synthesizer and singing along with his people. The song was performed in a giant yurt measuring 115 feet (35 metres) in height and 230 feet (70 metres) in diameter. Not exactly "Happy", but a record is a record.

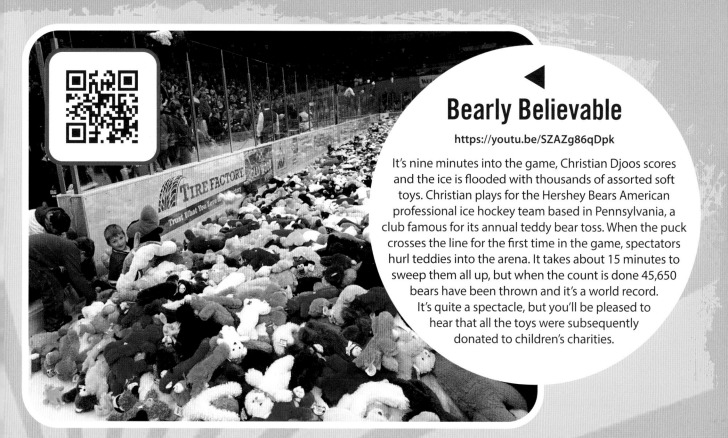

Bearly Believable

https://youtu.be/SZAZg86qDpk

It's nine minutes into the game, Christian Djoos scores and the ice is flooded with thousands of assorted soft toys. Christian plays for the Hershey Bears American professional ice hockey team based in Pennsylvania, a club famous for its annual teddy bear toss. When the puck crosses the line for the first time in the game, spectators hurl teddies into the arena. It takes about 15 minutes to sweep them all up, but when the count is done 45,650 bears have been thrown and it's a world record. It's quite a spectacle, but you'll be pleased to hear that all the toys were subsequently donated to children's charities.

▼ Flying the Flag

http://y2u.be/GwhtFvUShto

India's rivalry with Pakistan is often hostile but, in December 2014, the stakes were raised when India stole the world record for the largest human flag from their neighbours. Over 50,000 volunteers began gathering at 5.00am in the YMCA ground in Chennai, but it wasn't until noon that they were in position to form the tri-colour flag. Pakistan's previous record was just short of 29,000 – they've probably already started working on recapturing the title.

▼ Ever So Elfish

http://y2u.be/lu8dsjoW5-o

Nearly two thousand Santa's little helpers, aged between nine and 15, put on red, green and white hats, matching T-shirts and pointy plastic elf ears, and formed up outside a shopping mall in Bangkok. Those participating were required to stand still for 10 minutes with their elf ears and hats on. Some didn't make it and others were disqualified for not putting on their elf ears, but 1,792 correctly attired and standing still were enough to set a new record.

RECORD-
BREAKING
NUMBER OF
ELVES

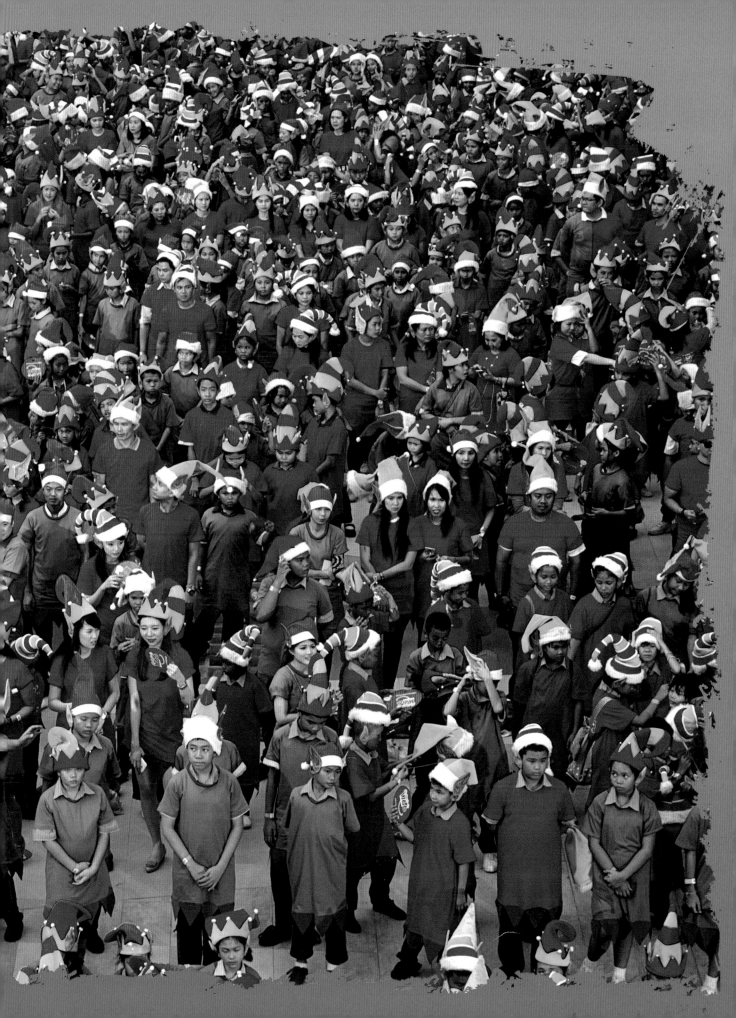

RECORD-BREAKING DOGS

It's dog beat dog in the competition for canine records. You'll love these proud pooches as they show off their record-breaking skills.

PEANUT

THE UGLIEST DOG IN THE WORLD

◀ Ugly Mutt

http://y2u.be/7AkYSGllKTk

Two-year-old Peanut, a mutt who is suspected of being a Chihuahua/Shitzu mix, doesn't have a lot going for him. He was seriously burned as a puppy and lived in an animal shelter for nine months before he found a home. On the looks side, he has matted hair, protruding teeth and looks as much rodent as canine. However, Peanut found fame in California in 2014. In a hotly contested competition, he swept the floor with the other hideous hounds and was crowned the World's Ugliest Dog.

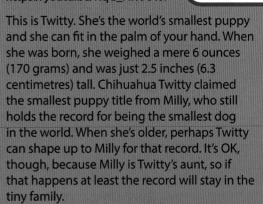

Puppy Love

https://youtu.be/HqG_AW9oVJl

This is Twitty. She's the world's smallest puppy and she can fit in the palm of your hand. When she was born, she weighed a mere 6 ounces (170 grams) and was just 2.5 inches (6.3 centimetres) tall. Chihuahua Twitty claimed the smallest puppy title from Milly, who still holds the record for being the smallest dog in the world. When she's older, perhaps Twitty can shape up to Milly for that record. It's OK, though, because Milly is Twitty's aunt, so if that happens at least the record will stay in the tiny family.

Ball Hog

https://youtu.be/9fUsPE0KrWQ

Finley the golden retriever is a bit of an Instagram star, as well as a record-breaker. His @FinnyBoyMolloy account, which has around 50,000 followers, is full of photos of the handsome dog from Canandaigua in New York State. It becomes pretty clear that Finley likes a ball – and often two or more balls at a time. OK, six-year-old Finley is ball-obsessed. He is rarely without one and will collect any that are thrown for him. Through hours of practice he has developed his unique skill: he can carry six tennis balls in his mouth at once. And doesn't he look proud?

▲ Dog Has His Day

http://y2u.be/29NPJDf2qto

As the runt of the litter, nobody expected Freddy to reach any great height. Now five years old, the Great Dane has been crowned the tallest dog in the world. This big, friendly giant measures 41 inches (104.14 cm) from his paws to his shoulders, and stands 7 feet and 6 inches (2.29 metres) when on his hind legs. A resident of Leigh-on-Sea in Essex, UK, Freddy is one hungry hound and scoffs down 2.2 lbs (1 kg) of minced beef, 8.8 oz (250 g) of steak and about 10.5 oz (300 g) of liver every day, although he also has a penchant for chicken, peanut butter – and sofas!

▲ All Ears

https://youtu.be/xsuXKAoqGn0

If Lou's ears flap every time someone views this video there must be quite a breeze in his neighbourhood, because this three-year-old, black and tan Coonhound's ears are each 13.38 inches (33.99 centimetres) long and the video's been watched over 1.5 million times. Since receiving the record in 2021, this adorable dog has become quite a star in her home state of Oregon. Coonhounds, traditionally tracking dogs, are known for their long ears, which are good for picking up smells and stirring up scents as they drag along the ground. Lou's owner also points out another advantage: she can lick her own ears clean if they get too dirty!

ENDURING PASSION

Breaking records can require years of grooming, hundreds of hours of practice, meticulous arrangement or serious organization skills. And some just happen in an instance of pure chance.

▶ The Uber

http://y2u.be/YR6Wh2Zy9jE

Uber driver Anthony struck lucky – or possibly unlucky – when he picked up Jimmy Donaldson in North Carolina. For Jimmy Donaldson is also Mr Beast, a YouTuber famous for such jinks as counting to 100,000 and tipping pizza-delivery guys $10,000. Mr Beast was looking for a ride to California on the west coast – a mere 2,256 miles (3,630 kilometres) away. Once Anthony had checked with his wife and called in sick at work, the longest Uber trip ever was on – and it was going to cost a beastly $5,500.

LONGEST UBER JOURNEY EVER

Sweet Stack

https://youtu.be/2WfRRib3IeQ

Just as, given an infinite amount of time, a monkey could apparently write a Shakespeare play, so with enough downtime can humans break world records. Take Will Cutbill from Solihull in the UK. He got so bored on a rainy day during the third Covid lockdown that he looked at the bag of M&M's he was eating, checked out the record for balancing them on top of each other and set out to beat it. It's no 100-metre sprint or daredevil cliff dive, but beating the record of four took patience and determination – and the will power not to eat your last five M&M's.

Eggs Over Easy

https://youtu.be/egbtNFWj-SA

Three? Just three? This must be one of the lowest records ever set, but it just goes to prove how difficult it is. Mohammed Muqbel from Yemen, succeeded in balancing three chicken's eggs in a vertical tower in Kuala Lumpur, Malaysia, and – essential to gain the record – left them to remain standing for more than five seconds. Mohammed had to be egg-xact and egg-ceptional in his balancing skills, judging where each egg's centre of mass was and ensuring they stacked perfectly. If you try this at home, make sure there's a soft landing – you don't want to end up with egg on your face!

FASTEST VIOLINIST IN THE WORLD

▲ On the Fiddle

http://y2u.be/PA_1oS8Ch4U

Record holder Ben Lee is no novelty violinist. He was a child prodigy; a student at the London School of Music; played with the Arctic Monkeys, McFly and others; and eventually formed successful rock violin duo Fuse. In the summer of 2009, Lee suffered damage to his right hand and wrist after being run over by a truck while cycling. To inspire his rehabilitation, his bandmate challenged him to break the world record for fastest violinist. In fact, he went on to break the record five times, on both acoustic and electric violin.

It's Da Bomb!

https://youtu.be/fODeb-XvOBc

Bath bombs are the ultimate in good, clean fun, right? Lob one into your bath and it fizzes madly, colours the water and smells delicious. Gift website VAT19 decided to build the world's biggest bath bomb – around a hundred times bigger than the normal ping-pong or tennis ball-sized one you'd use at home. Watch as they scale up the normal ingredients – corn starch, citric acid, baking soda and dye – and make a 2000-lb (900 kg) bath bomb. It's so big they have to roll it into their "bath" (a swimming pool), but is it worth the effort?

AMAZING ATHLETES

Every sport has its record breakers. These stars, whether from well-known sports like football and swimming, or less well-known, like balloon-batting, have some amazing achievements to crow about!

Aye Aye Skipper

https://youtu.be/kOT19pRZ5rE

A small, flat piece of grey stone bounces along a stretch of open water at top speed – a beautiful, awe-inspiring sight. Scotsman Dougie Isaacs has skipped – or skimmed – a stone further than anybody else in the world. Everyone's had a go at the beach, but to do it well requires surprising physical effort and incredible skill. When Dougie's stone finally stutters and sinks, it has travelled an astonishing 399.6 feet (121.8 metres), which is the world distance record for stone skipping.

▼ Ride 'Em Cowboy

https://youtu.be/zn1v-603CO0

It was the showdown the rodeo world was waiting for as reigning World Champion, Jose Vitor Leme from Brazil, mounted Woopaa, the number one-ranked bull. In professional bull riding, judges mark the rider on control and the bull on style of movement, agility and speed, with 50 points available for each. As Woopaa high-kicked, twisted and bucked for all he was worth, Leme remained in complete control for the required eight seconds. The crowd went as wild as Woopaa, but was it enough for a world-record points total for bull and rider?

RECORD-BREAKING RODEO RIDE

▶ Time on his Hands

https://youtu.be/xc5-nk5z8FU

Twenty-four-year-old American Zion Clark is an inspiration to us all. He was born with no lower body due to a rare condition known as caudal regression syndrome, but he has never let his condition slow him down. Living by his motto of "No excuses", Zion became a pro-wrestler and a motivational speaker before taking the world record for the fastest human on two hands in a 20-metre run. He is now aiming to become the first American athlete to compete in both the Olympic (wrestling) and Paralympic (wheelchair racing) games in 2024 – and few would doubt this phenomenal athlete's chances of success.

▼ Jump at the Chance

http://y2u.be/kPZvtIDLjpI

This is an unofficial world record, but there appears no reason to doubt it – and it is exceptional. It features Kevin Bania, a CrossFit athlete (CrossFit is a sport featuring weightlifting, sprinting and jumping exercises). Bania attempts a record standing box jump, which involves jumping onto a box or level surface. From a standing start, he leaps from the floor to a platform 5 feet, 4.5 inches (1.63 metres) high. Bania himself stands 5 feet, 10 inches (1.78 metres) tall, so he is within six inches (15 cm) of jumping his own height.

THE MAN WHO JUMPS ALMOST AS HIGH AS HIMSELF

WILD SPORTS

Terrified by the high board at the pool? Dizzy on the top storey of the multi-storey car park? Then perhaps you should just sit down and watch some people who know no fear ...

▼ New Ball Game

http://y2u.be/NehU-6NCBco

Zorbing is the sport of rolling down a hill in the kind of plastic sphere given to bored hamsters. Protected by a pocket of air between them and the edges of the ball, the participants can thrust the ball forward but have limited control over the direction. Miguel Ferrero from Spain, nicknamed "The Adventurer", was encased in a Zorb ball and threw himself down a ski run at La Molina in the Pyrenees. He reached a record speed of 31.2mph (50.2km/h).

THE FASTEST ZORBING ON RECORD

◀ Extreme Swimming

http://y2u.be/IJY8VgmvXHc

Diana Nyad became the first person to swim the 100 miles (160 kilometres) from Cuba to Florida without a protective shark cage. Braving rough seas, the fear of shark attack, vomiting from salt-water intake and wearing a heavy suit to withstand jellyfish stings, Diana succeeded on her fifth attempt over 35 years – her fourth since turning 60.

Snow Business

http://y2u.be/ztWX5ynl06g

France's Edmond Plawczyk had waited a long time to reclaim his snowboarding speed record. He had originally set the world record in 1997, but that was broken in 1999. April 2015 was payback time as Edmond donned his strange-looking, red-winged suit and aerodynamic helmet at the top of the slopes of the famous Chabrières piste in the French Alps. He was soon flying down the 4,600-foot (1,400 metre) course, which at one point measured a gradient of 98 per cent, to realise his ambition and a new record speed of 126.309 mph (203.275 km/h). Sweet.

▼ Water Wall

https://youtu.be/-ucBfEDVJbA

Woah! This wave is bigger than a house. In fact, this wave is bigger than a 12-story block of flats and Briton Tom Butler is riding it. The location is Praia do Norte beach, near the fishing village of Nazaré in Portugal. It's a place which is known for its massive swells, but this one was really massive. In fact, observers estimated the height of this particular wave as more than 100 feet (30.5 metres) high. It's certainly pretty intimidating – scary even – and afterwards Tom admitted that surfing it was like "running away from a raging bull".

THE LARGEST WAVE EVER SURFED

TRULY REMARKABLE

It's a wonderful record-breaking world and YouTube contributors across the globe are out filming every remarkable event and achievement.

Balancing Act

https://youtu.be/alfFKxrIxy8

Jenga can be the most nerve-wracking and frustrating game. If you've ever played it yourself, you'll know that the tension as you remove a brick – and wait to see if the structure is going to collapse –can be excruciating. Captain Noodles here wouldn't worry too much about taking on you or me, though, because he's a master of balance. This video shows him building his record-breaking tower of 518 bricks (made shortly after his friend set a record of 517), with them all perched on a single brick as a base. Now bearing in mind there are 54 bricks in a normal box, it stacks up to quite a feat.

▼ Pop-Up Painting

http://y2u.be/BV4Vj8Je3bQ

In June 2014, world-famous Chinese artist Yang Yongchun unveiled a special piece of art. Named *Rhythms of Youth*, it depicted the impressive architectural landscape of Nanjing and the Yangtze River that runs through it. Not only was it the largest and longest street painting in the world, measuring an astonishing 1,200 feet (365 metres) long and covering 28,000 sq. feet (2,600 sq. metres), but it was also an anamorphic painting – created in a distorted manner to make it appear three-dimensional.

THE LONGEST STREET PAINTING

► A Fine Line

http://y2u.be/y4VJssQv_Qw

Domino-line topples – you either love them or you hate them. If you fall into the latter category, best move along. For the rest of us, there is something hypnotic and satisfying about dominoes falling one by one. This is a single line, so no effects, no dominoes lifted by cranes or toppled by balls – just straightforward domino action. And, after spending two days putting 15,524 multi-coloured dominoes in line and initiating a 5-minute toppling sequence, professional domino artist Lily Hevesh earned the record for the longest domino line ever. Exquisite.

LONGEST LINE OF DOMINOES EVER TOPPLED

▼ Mummy Mia

https://youtu.be/60ljsBZ-Ltl

This is one of those that falls into the category of mind-bendingly pointless but nonetheless makes your jaw drop. Here we have a reproduction of the famous death mask of the boy pharaoh Tutankhamun, but in black and white rather than the familiar blue and gold. That's because it's made from cups of coffee – a staggering 7,260 of them. It also took 143 pounds (65 kilograms) of coffee, 1,760 pints (1,000 litres) of milk, 5,279 pints (3,000 litres) of water and 12 hours to set the record. But was it de-coffin-ated…?

▼ A Real Blast

http://y2u.be/iFC8hFci2kl

The best firework displays always keep something special back for the grand finale of the show. The display for the Feast of St Catherine in Zurrieq, Malta, certainly didn't disappoint. The crowds that had gathered at one of the island's biggest festivals witnessed the spectacle of the world's single biggest firework. The rocket, called the *ballun tal-blalen* (which loosely translates as "balloon of balls"), exploded from a 10-foot-wide (3-metre) shell weighing 570 pounds (260 kilograms), launching a chain reaction that saw the whole sky covered in chrysanthemum-pattern lights. Enjoy – it may not last long, but the brief effect is completely dazzling.

◀ Balloon Loon

https://youtu.be/giKqzGGcq8E

The unwritten law of record breaking is that if it's dangerous enough, someone will try it. Here's 26-year-old Remi Ouvrard who took to the skies over Chatellerault, western France, in a balloon piloted by his father. Rather than standing in the basket as normal, Remi sat on a metal chair on top of the inflated canvas sphere and as it rose more than 3,280 feet (1,000 metres) above sea level, the daredevil stood up and danced. There wasn't even a record to break in this category but, thanks to Remi, there is now!

IT TAKES ALL SORTS

Isn't it a wonderful record-breaking world when a footballing cyclist and a martial arts champion can share a page with the world's largest scooter?

▼ On My Head!

http://y2u.be/joA086aXDlk

As a Nigerian footballer in Cambodia, the possibility existed that Harrison Chinedu might have got overlooked by the national team's coaches. But Harrison was hard to miss when, kitted out in the national strip, he rode a bicycle from a beach outside Nigeria's capital Lagos all the way into the city to the national stadium. Oh, did I forget to say that he did the whole 64 miles (103 kilometres) balancing a football on his head? Six months earlier, his record walk with a ball on his head (28.84 miles/48.04 kilometres) had been quickly broken, so this time he's hoping he's in the record books to stay.

RECORD FOOTBALL BALANCING ACT

▼ Everybody Freeze!

https://youtu.be/tzCzXuLZYLE

Autumn 2016 and a new craze was sweeping the Internet: the Mannequin Challenge. Across numerous platforms, people shared videos of groups acting as if they had been frozen in time. Perhaps the most famous video came from the White House and featured Bruce Springsteen, Tom Hanks, Diana Ross and others (you can view it on YouTube). Of course, competition for the biggest Mannequin Challenge was soon on, with pride of place going to this magnificent effort by 55,000 spectators, players, staff and paramedics at a Cape Town sevens rugby tournament in South Africa's Cape Town Stadium.

WORLD'S LARGEST MANNEQUIN CHALLENGE

Out of his Tree

https://youtu.be/0D2nCEv_9tY

With his bowl cut haircut and 80s outfits it's difficult to take Oliver Tree seriously. But that's the way the musician and comedian likes it. His love of scooters, however, does seem genuine: he was a pro rider in high school and his breakthrough hit, 'Hurt', concerned a crash that broke both his wrists. To promote his latest album, Tree was back on a scooter for a record-breaking attempt. He aimed to ride the world's biggest kick scooter – a strange contraption that's a massive 13 feet, 7.9 inches (4.16 metres) tall and 10 feet, 3.6 inches (3.13 metres) long. The skit is hard to believe, but it's there on the certificate.

Over and Out

https://youtu.be/YJsKFEWT_E0

Xie Desheng is a martial arts champion and he's pretty handy with a pair of sticks connected by a short chain otherwise known as "nunchucks". He moves along a line of candles with – it's the only way to describe it – ninja-like precision, extinguishing flame after flame as he goes. It's mesmerising and he puts out 52 candles in just 60 seconds, which why he's the world record-holder at this discipline. Incidentally, in some countries nunchucks are considered offensive weapons and it's illegal to own or to use them – you have been warned…

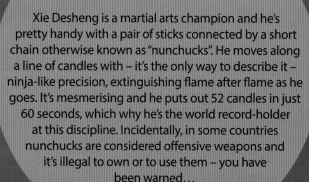

▼ Pulling Faces

https://youtu.be/5GFn09SmbxU

Tang Shuquan of Chengdu City, China, spends a lot of time hoping the wind doesn't change direction and he stays "like that". Named the King of Deformed Faces, Tang spent 10 years working on being able to contort his face into the ugliest shapes possible. After winning the world record for gurning, Tang, who has the extraordinary ability of biting his own nose, even challenged all-comers – offering a £10,000 prize to anyone who can match his face-stretching skills.

THE GURNING WORLD CHAMPION

MAD MOVIE RECORDS

Roll the credits! From Bollywood to Hollywood, the glamorous and exciting world of the movies lists the famous and the not so famous in its annals of achievement.

MOST VIEWED MOVIE TRAILER

▲ Spider Trail

https://youtu.be/rt-2cxAiPJk

2019's *Avengers: Endgame* looked to have set records that could last forever. Less than two years later, however, along came *Spider-Man: No Way Home,* which immediately smashed its record for the most viewed movie trailer in a day. The preview of the third instalment of the *Spider-Man* series racked up an incredible 355.5 million views across all online platforms in just its first 24 hours. That was over 60 million more than the *Avengers* trailer and it was all the more impressive as an earlier trailer had been leaked, ruining intended surprises such as the appearances of Electro, Green Goblin and Doc Ock.

A Dress to Impress

https://youtu.be/ZaCGSGekmWg

On 19 May 1962, during the 45th-birthday celebrations for President John F. Kennedy, actress Marilyn Monroe sashayed onto the stage at Madison Square Garden, took off her fur coat and famously sang "Happy Birthday, Mr President". Under that fur coat Marilyn was wearing a sheer, sequinned dress so tight that she had to be sewed into it. It was an era-defining moment. Fast-forward 54 years and that same dress is under the hammer at auction. It was bought by Ripley's Believe It or Not for an incredible $4.8 million (£3.7 m), making it the most expensive dress ever.

THE WORLD'S TINIEST MOVIE EVER "FILMED"

▲ Minute Movie

http://y2u.be/oSCX78-8-q0

Like many great movies, *A Boy and His Atom* has a heart-warming friendship at its centre and – no spoilers here – a moving ending. It has been watched over 6 million times since it was uploaded in 2013, which is particularly astounding as it can't really be seen by the human eye. IBM researchers used a scanning, tunnelling microscope to move thousands of carbon-monoxide molecules (two atoms stacked on top of each other) to make a film so small it can be seen only when you magnify it 100 million times. It's the world's smallest stop-motion movie.

Extra Special

http://y2u.be/miuzO4yI0V4

Acclaimed director Richard Attenborough faced a real challenge when filming *Gandhi* on location in India in 1980. He was determined to re-create the great man's life as accurately as possible and had to film a funeral scene in which a million people had lined the route. Attenborough chose to film on the thirty-third anniversary of Gandhi's funeral and managed to recruit around 300,000 volunteers and actors – the most extras ever to appear in a feature film.

The Car's the Star

https://youtu.be/I5qKCpqNBwo

If anything qualifies as a genuine movie icon it's this 1968 Ford Mustang GT, as driven at break-neck speed through the streets of San Francisco by Steve McQueen in the famous film, *Bullitt*. Having been used as a family runaround, the car had been sitting in a garage for over 30 years, but in early 2020 it came up for auction. Normally this particular model in this sort of condition would be worth about $25,000, but it went for a gobsmacking $3.74 million.

TRANSPORT RECORDS

This collection of the bizarre, brilliant, marvellous and downright silly means of transport would get some strange looks down the High Street.

Life in the Fast Lane

https://youtu.be/CTgLnUgzZYk

It's got a bar of Turkish Delight as a gear stick, the indicators are flashing flower pots and the speedometer is a mantelpiece clock. It's quite a sight and people certainly stare when this sofa on wheels takes to the road. Mind you, the glances aren't always admiring – but perhaps that's the less-than-tasteful furry fake leopard skin it's covered in. According to that mantelpiece clock, it does 90 mph (145 km/h), which makes it the fastest sofa in the world!

THE WORLD'S FASTEST BARROW

Wheelbarrow Hero

https://youtu.be/a-CoDUevJiQ

After building the world's fastest shed, which he drove at over 100 mph (160 km/h), Kevin Nicks looked around for another record-breaking challenge. Stuck in lockdown, he chose to build a zero-budget machine only using things he had lying around, starting with a clapped-out old moped. With a bit of tinkering, he assembled the perfect accompaniment to his high-powered shed – the fastest ever wheelbarrow. Named the "Barrow of Speed", it's a motorised three-wheeler that you drive while standing on a footrest. Now a wheelbarrow is a pretty unstable thing to push around the garden, so imagine what it feels like taking it past 40 mph (65 km/h).

One-Wheeled Wonder

http://y2u.be/Jzeq7FWl3Dg

The idea behind the monowheel is simple: build a big enough wheel and you can fit a person inside. Motorized monowheels have been around since the 1930s, but issues with balance, steering and visibility make them dangerous to ride. Kevin Scott built his monowheel, *War Horse*, from a 200cc go-kart engine. It has a diameter of 59 inches (1.5 metres) and the only way to change direction is by leaning. Nevertheless, in September 2016, in Yorkshire, England, Kev rode along an airstrip and back, clocking up a record speed of 61 mph (98.5 km/h).

◢ Poor Man's Porsche

https://youtu.be/OgImEeX8-PI

A casual glance at the race track footage might reveal a sleek silver Porsche 911 elegantly speeding along in slow motion. A closer look, however, will confirm that the Ferdinand GT3 RS is not that. It's actually a bike covered with a sports car chassis that's coated in silver foil – and that isn't slow motion, it's real time (watch to the end to see the moment the real thing speeds by). Austrian artist Hannes Langeder is the creator and "driver" of the Ferdinand, the world's slowest Porsche, and his deadpan presentation makes for an hilarious five-minute super car video.

WORLD'S HEAVIEST WORKING BICYCLE

▲ Heavy Going

http://y2u.be/Zm3ROyV1dhA

You won't see this kind of bike steaming up Alpe D'Huez in the Tour de France, but Frank Dose's extraordinary vehicle is already a winner. The bike, which took him six months to build, broke the record for the heaviest bike in the world, weighing in at over one tonne. Despite the fact that it sports 5-foot (1.53-metre) diameter tyres from an industrial fertiliser spreader, a frame made from scrap steel and a beer-crate saddle, Frank still managed to pedal the required 328 feet (100 metres) to earn himself the record.

BIZARRE PEOPLE

The say: "If you've got it, flaunt it." None of these record breakers seems to have any problem flaunting their special features. And, as you will discover, they are pretty special ...

▼ Hair Style

https://youtu.be/HYjmLzu76J0

Life as a record-breaker isn't always about triumph. It can be a burden. Larry Gomez from San Bernardino, California, was born with the incredibly rare disorder hypertrichosis, which resulted in 98 per cent of his body – including his face – being coated in hair. Despite being bullied as a child, Larry refused to hide away and developed an incredibly positive attitude to his differences. Now married and running his own business, he proudly admits to being "the hairiest man in the world" and uses his own experience to inspire others to be confident in their own appearance.

WORLD'S HAIRIEST FACE

◀ The Eyes Have It

http://y2u.be/8n14AmSWbAg

The average person's eyelashes measure 0.4 inches (1 cm) or so. They do their job of protecting the eye pretty well. Some people apply alluring false eyelashes, which extend their length to around 0.6 inches (1.5 cm), but Shanghai-born You Jianxia has eyelashes that reach an incredible five inches (12 cm). They hang down the side of her eyes to her mouth like jungle vines or delicate school-gym climbing ropes. You claims her lashes only began to grow after she retired from her high-status finance post and started spending more time in her garden, and she credits the amazing length to being at one with nature.

▶ That's Nailed It!

https://youtu.be/Zr7cnS2P1mA

Texas-born Ayana Williams's journey to fame began with a simple dare: a friend challenged her to grow her fingernails longer than three inches (7.6 centimetres). More than 20 years later, she still hasn't cut them and each of her nails has grown over 15 inches (40 centimetres) long. In fact, she has a total of nearly 19 feet (5.7 metres) of nail. She admits that having such long nails brings its own problems: she uses a pencil to type on the computer, has to be careful her nails don't get caught in the steering wheel when driving and can't tie her own shoelaces!

Back to Front Boy

http://y2u.be/63h81dNRwRs

It was at a Minecraft conference in 2015 that 14-year-old Maxwell Day revealed his unique skill. Having seen a photo of the record-holder for largest foot rotation, he was soon demonstrating that he could rotate his right foot 157 degrees and turn his left foot round by 143 degrees, easily breaking the previous record of 120 degrees. Maxwell, from Enfield in the UK, asserts that he feels no pain when rotating his feet and he is able to walk with them rotated (although not fast enough to claim that record – yet).

EXTREME EATING

The world of competitive eating is not for the faint-hearted or for those brought up not to shovel down their food. But it is pretty amazing ...

Clear the Table

https://youtu.be/nVyPs3R9dZY

SUPER FAST FOOD

Leah Shutkever is Britain's greatest speed eater. "Shuteater", as she calls herself, will shovel down any foodstuff in huge quantities if there's a record waiting at the end of it. In 2020, she undertook an all-out attack on the speed-eating record books, including scoffing ten jam doughnuts in three minutes, eight tomatoes in a minute and a cucumber in less than 30 seconds, as well as drinking 1.7 pints (1 litre) of gravy in just over a minute. They are all available to watch on her YouTube channel, but this is a good "taster" as she attempts to consume 12 sausages in under a minute.

I Scream, You Scream...

https://youtu.be/EaHrWPkWtOU

There was no brain freeze for Miki Sudo when she attended the first ever World Ice Cream Eating Championship at the Indiana State Fair in Indianapolis in 2017. Miki scoffed down 16.5 pints (9.38 litres) of vanilla ice cream in just six minutes. That's equivalent to around 28 large tubs of frozen deliciousness. Miki, of course, has form for this kind of thing. She is currently the top-ranked female competitive eater in the US and holds the records for fastest time to eat 50 Creme Eggs (6 minutes, 15 seconds) and chugging a gallon (4.5 litres) of milk before sky diving (54.25 seconds).

▶ Sprout About It

http://y2u.be/7Jl8gf2V98U

For many people, Brussels sprouts represent the unacceptable side of Christmas dinner, left on the side when all else has been polished off. Not for Emma Dalton, though. The surprisingly slim 27-year-old competitive eater, who has stuffed back a 5,000-calorie burger in under 10 minutes, has worked her way through the world's biggest helping of sprouts. In one sitting lasting just over half an hour, she scoffed 325 of the mini cabbages – that's almost 7 pounds (3 kilograms) of festive veg. Mind you, not even Emma seems to actually like sprouts, as she coated them in mint sauce, gravy and ketchup to help wash them down.

WORLD RECORD BRUSSELS SPROUTS EATER

▶ Cockney Chow-Down

https://youtu.be/MBAOiKg45WU

Pie and mash is a traditional dish of the East End of London. It is as Cockney as pearly kings and queens or a knees-up around the ol' joanna. In September 2020, Max Stanford earned his place as an honorary Cockney by eating his way through 18 mince beef pies and seven portions of mash and liquor (the accompanying green parsley sauce). His massive plate contained food weighing a total of 11 pounds (5 kilos) and Max set a world record by demolishing the lot in just 43 minutes. That's one enormous portion of "Lilley and Skinner" (dinner), as the locals might say!

Blowing Bubbles

http://y2u.be/hjPLFYju7KI

Champion bubble blower Chad Fell of Alabama blew a bubblegum bubble with a diameter of 20 inches (50.8 centimetres) that remained intact for a full five seconds. It was no fluke. Chad takes his skill seriously. He gets through two bags of Dubble Bubble a week in practice and knows his science. He drinks cold water to regulate the temperature in his mouth and chews for 15 minutes to cut down the sugar to aid elasticity before carefully adding air.

▼ Oh, Crumbs

http://y2u.be/OZMMSW4Ackk

Many of the records in this book are impossible for readers to try at home. They are either dangerous, expensive, require specific skills or are just too gross. So here's one you can have a go at yourself. All you need is a chocolate muffin and a camera. Watch the video, study the tactics of Kyle Thomas Moyer of Pennsylvania, USA, who set the record for the fastest time to eat a muffin without using your hands, and prepare your attempt. The target to beat is 28.18 seconds, and remember: no hands!

On a Roll

https://youtu.be/cb9mldUPB2o

Joey Chestnut has earned his place in history for his prestigious eating exploits at the annual Nathan's Hot Dog contests, but he is no one-snack pony. In 2020, Joey rang out for a delivery and settled down for an attempt on one of the iconic world records in competitive eating: the most Big Macs eaten by one person in a single sitting. Unfazed by the huge pile of 32 burgers, rolls and garnish (and no, he definitely didn't want fries with that!), Joey tucks in – will he manage to take the record or will the dreaded "meat sweats" take their toll?

▶ King of the Desert

https://youtu.be/N7Gp8Mqko70

The Dakar Rally is the biggest motor rally in the world and considered to be the most dangerous too – over 70 competitors, support staff and spectators have died since the race began in 1977. Its original route was Paris to Dakar in Senegal, but it has been held in various locations. Frenchman Stéphane Peterhansel first competed in the motorbike category in 1988. He won his first title in 1991 and triumphed in five of the next seven years, before swapping to the car category in 1999. In 2013, with his 11th Dakar win, he became the rally's most successful ever competitor, but he didn't stop there. In 2021, the 'Desert King' notched up his 14th victory.

MOST WINS IN THE DAKAR RALLY

NICE MOVES!

These entertaining clips pay homage to the hot-footers who have danced themselves into a pirouetting, head-spinning, pole-leaping, tip-tapping, mascot jiving, record-breaking world.

Lords of the Dance

https://youtu.be/dRE7rU4Ik-g

This video is a showcase for Fricska, a Hungarian folk dancing group. Maybe you're not that interested in folk dancing, but it's folk dancing with a modern twist, injected with incredible pace, and it's spectacular. These boys practise hard – they have the blisters to prove it – and among their achievements is the record for the fastest folk dance. However, their hitting and slapping is faster than the human eye can compute, so to verify their record attempt the judges had to watch it back in slow motion, but, yes, these dancers hit and slapped 3,937 times in two minutes.

▼ Body Popping

http://y2u.be/yHzpcBuQlpM

Julia Gunthel goes by the stage name Zlata. A 27-year-old Russian living in Germany, she is also known as "the Most Flexible Woman on Earth". Watching the way she twists and bends her body around, it is hard to imagine that Julia actually has a spine. Her balloon-bursting act just has to be seen to be believed. She manages to burst three balloons in 12 seconds, using the curve of her back as a press. That just can't be comfortable.

▶ Human Propeller

http://y2u.be/EZfVAxG2-h4

The headspin, a staple power move of breakdancing, is a routine where the dancer's body is rotated while standing on his head. Just watch the poise and strength of 23-year-old Aichi Ono of Japan as it seems he tries to screw his head into the ground. "The Human Tornado", or "Spinboy" as he is also called, spins at a breakneck speed, racking up an incredible 142 rotations in a minute on a TV show in Japan.

RECORD-BREAKING NUMBER OF HEADSPINS

Limbo Queen

http://y2u.be/tqI4NKLhhvU

Shemika Charles is the world-famous Limbo Queen. Ever since setting fire to the Guinness World Record for limbo-ing a mere 8.5 inches (21.5 centimetres) from the floor live on TV in 2010, Ms Charles has travelled the world, showing off her unique talent. In June 2015, however, the Limbo Queen took her skills to a whole new low – and limboed *under a car!* The first world record of its kind and genuinely unbelievable!

In a Spin

http://y2u.be/_U827SJO3Qw

Kinderdijk is famous for its 18th-century windmills – and now for the classic breakdance move that shares the name. More than 70 b-boys from the Netherlands, Italy and France gathered in front of the town's iconic structures to spin on their back and shoulders – a precarious move in the middle of the waterway. Nevertheless, they succeeded in setting a new world record for the number of simultaneous windmills performed in 30 seconds.

THAT'S GOTTA HURT!

"Now that has got to hurt." Sometimes you feel as if you are about to experience the pain yourself as you watch these record breakers undergo self-torture. Of course you aren't. Still, "Ouch!"

Yes He Can

https://youtu.be/I1ztoXgwsj4

They now call him "Can Head", but back when he was just plain Jamie Keeton he was watching a baseball match and happened to place a cold can of cola against his head to cool himself down. Surprisingly, he found the can stuck to his head. Jamie had discovered he had a unique talent – an ability to stick not just cans but any solid object to his head. Is he some kind of mutant? Is it to do with how he sweats on that bald pate? Whatever the science, it has made Jamie a record-breaker. He's managed ten cans at one time and that's going to take some beating.

A Changed Man

https://youtu.be/ETubeM1RRCM

With his greying hair and sensible glasses, it's just about possible to describe Rolf Buchholz as an ordinary-looking chap. However, the 60-year-old German has put himself through numerous agonies to make himself look pretty extraordinary. Rolf has made a record-breaking 516 alterations to his physical appearance, including covering 90 per cent of his body in tattoos, having subdermal implants (bumps inserted below the skin), two of which stick out of the top of his head like a pair of horns, and wearing 453 piercings, many of them in places that would make your eyes water!

▼ The Flame Game

http://y2u.be/cNuwX0hTFKU

When you take a spoonful of soup and realise slightly too late that it's still too hot for you, that soup is around 85°C. If you're unlucky, your tongue will be blistered for a day or two. Now consider Brad Byers, a man nicknamed the "Human Tool Box" (because he can insert tools through his nasal cavities, but that's another story). Brad trumps your hot soup by more than 20 times as he extinguishes a propane blow torch on his tongue. Incredibly, he's basically licking a 2,000°C flame – what on earth can his tongue be made of?

▶ Cold Storage

https://youtu.be/V9jqJ-1s_Fw

Putting yourself in a "state of daydreaming" is not your typical preparation for a record-breaking attempt, but that's exactly what Frenchman Romain Vandendorpe did to earn his place in the record books. What did he do? Oh yes, he was buried up to his neck in ice with no shirt in a plexiglass cabin for over two-and-a-half hours. Of course, you'll have to copy his other preparation exercises, which included spending hours in an ice-cold jacuzzi, training in a large freezer and being buried in snow. Maybe best to just reserve the daydreaming excuse for the next time you're caught not paying attention at school.

LONGEST DEEP FREEZE

◀ Heavy Metal

http://y2u.be/Rj7vKStJmtA

A living confusion of tattoo and glistening metal, Elaine Davidson is the world's most-pierced woman. A Brazilian-born nurse, living in Edinburgh, Elaine has 462 studs and rings (192 on her face), which saw her crowned the world's most-pierced woman in 2000. But Elaine didn't stop there – as of March 2012, she had amassed over 9,000 piercings. She never removes the rings and studs, which means she carries around an extra 6.6 pounds (3 kilograms). But you wouldn't miss her in a crowd!

THE WOMAN WITH THE MOST PIERCINGS

THE MOST EXPENSIVE

You'll be surprised at some of the things that turn up in the "most expensive" basket in the YouTube supermarket. Who would expect some scorpion venom next to a masterpiece?

◀ Lush Loo

https://youtu.be/-qLCHM51StY

Would you consider splashing out the million pounds this golden toilet is said to be worth? This ultimate bathroom throne has over 40,000 diamonds (335 carats' worth) encrusted in its seat – the highest number of diamonds set on a toilet – and is worth $1.28 million. The creators, Coronet Jewellery, are not expecting it to be graced by a VIP bottom anytime soon, though. They say it's a piece of artwork for exhibition only, but admit if a customer was feeling "flush", they might be willing to make a replica.

▶ Breaking the Banksy

https://youtu.be/eXKE0nAMmg4

It was the moment that shocked the whole art world. "Girl With Balloon", a famous work by British artist Banksy, had just been sold for over £1 million. However, as the hammer fell, the painting was sucked into a shredder that had been hidden in its ornate, gilded frame. Banksy later revealed he had secretly built a shredder into the frame years before, in anticipation of this moment. Ironically, the picture was estimated to be worth up to 50 percent more in its shredded state. It might be some time before we witness a faster destruction of a million-pound masterpiece.

THE MOST EXPENSIVE WORK OF ART

◀ Sting in the Tale

https://youtu.be/E-TOB9DglPg

The list of the most expensive liquids on earth is fascinating: perfume, champagne and human blood are all predictably on the list; there are some surprises like maple syrup and nasal spray; and no computer user would be surprised to see printer ink near the top at around $8,000 a gallon (4.5 litres). Just be thankful, then, that you don't need too much scorpion venom (used in anti-cancer drugs). Scorpions are difficult and dangerous to obtain and milk (see the video!) and their venom fetches an amazing $40 million a gallon.

▼ Prize Fries

https://youtu.be/ZwF304u6Edc

"Cheap as chips" is the saying. Well, these chips are anything but. New York City's iconic Serendipity 3 restaurant has been a foodie's fantasy for over 60 years, revelling in its reputation for decadence and playfulness. So, in honour of National French Fry Day (who knew there was one?) on 13 June 2021, they set about creating the world's most expensive French fries. Their Crème de la Crème Pomme Frites are blanched in champagne, thrice cooked in pure goose fat from Southwest France and seasoned with truffle salt, topped with shaved truffle and finally sprinkled with edible gold dust. Oh what's that? How much? A mere $200 a portion.

Gold Caller

https://youtu.be/gl62BSjp7Vo

Plated in 24-carat gold, studded with 137 diamonds and with an intricate watch mechanism on the back, this is no ordinary iPhone 11 Pro. Watch as YouTuber Marques Brownlee unboxes the most expensive iPhone in the world. It's available in a limited edition of just one and costs $100,000, so you'll need to save up, but console yourself with the fact that the ticking from the watch would probably be really annoying when you're making a call and all that gold makes it far too heavy to carry around with you…

THE MOST EXPENSIVE CHIPS

A LONG WAY DOWN

Some people just have no respect for the laws of gravity. It might have kept sensible folk's feet on the ground for centuries, but not your adrenaline-junkie record breaker ...

Leap of Faith

https://youtu.be/rvKj79d3Hr8

They call it "death diving". The name doesn't inspire confidence, does it? The discipline requires divers to jump in belly flop position, opening their bodies and spreading their arms and legs, and only adopt a streamlined diving position at the last second. Reaching a speed of over 60 miles per hour (97 kph), if they get their timing even slightly wrong, hitting the water is like slamming into a brick wall. Yet all that just encourages adrenaline junkies like Norwegian Ken Stornes. In 2021, he threw himself off a 102-foot (31-metre) tall cliff, making it easily the highest death dive ever.

Jump de Triomphe

http://y2u.be/MLejkyXbJlc

Australian motorcycle stunt rider Robbie Maddison likes a New Year's Eve party; his record-breaking end-of-year stunts have become a tradition for the thrill-seeker. Few of them can beat the 2008 effort when the 27-year-old sped his bike off a 35-foot (10-metre) high ramp to the top of the 96-foot (30-metre) high replica of the Arc de Triomphe in Las Vegas. Having set the world record for the highest motorcycle jump, he then plunged the 80-foot (24-metre) drop back – breaking his hand in the process.

THE FASTEST BARE-HAND CLIMBER

▼ Look Mum, Just Hands!

http://y2u.be/Wy3SuhEQHVg

Dan Osman was the fastest bare-handed speed climber in the world. In this ascent, he climbs Bears Reach, a 400-foot (122-metre) rock face of Lover's Leap in California, in just 4 minutes, 25 seconds. He uses no ropes or grips, just gaining hold with his feet and his bare hands. Osman held other mountain-stunt world records, including a freefall rope jump of 1,100 feet (335 metres) at the Leaning Tower in Yosemite, California. Sadly, this was also the spot where he met his death after a tragic rope malfunction.

Joy Ride

https://youtu.be/gA0zzD55qKM

Austrian stuntman Günter Schachermayr loves his Vespa scooter. He goes everywhere on it, not just to the shops. He's parachuted from a plane on it, jumped out of a balloon from 20,000 feet (6,096 metres) on it, and launched himself on a bungee on it, so it was no surprise to see him try some parascending on it. Attached to a parachute by a 300-foot (90-metre) rope and towed by a 380 horsepower (283 kilowatt) powerboat, he and his beloved 320-pound (145-kilogram) scooter take to the air at a record height of 245 feet (75 metres) above Lake Wolfgang in Austria.

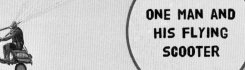

ONE MAN AND HIS FLYING SCOOTER

▲Walking the Walk

http://y2u.be/9W0umbacmzg

In China, Adili Wuxor is known as the "prince of tightrope walking", so his special skill won't be a surprise. The feat itself might impress, though. The 45-year-old Wuxor breaks his own record by walking a wire that's 5,905 feet (1,800 metres) long and about 590 feet (180 metres) above the ground across the Yellow River. He pauses at the centre for over half an hour, performing various stunts on the 1.5-inch-thick wire (3.6-centimetre) as he waits for his assistant, who started at the other end. He then proceeds to walk over him and continues his epic walk to the end of the wire.

COOL CONSTRUCTIONS

The world of engineering deserves a special mention in the record-breaking hall of fame. The world's greatest tunnels and bridges are spectacular examples of human achievement.

▶ Bridge of Size

http://y2u.be/WP1rZrB9SZI

Opened in 2009, the Sidu River Bridge in Hubei Province of China is the highest bridge in the world. It is a suspension bridge that hangs a vertiginous 1,600 feet (496 metres) above the river gorge. It spans just over 5,000 feet (1,5124 metres) across the river valley; far enough that builders had to use a rocket to string the first pilot line. Some claim it is also the only bridge in the world high enough for a person to reach terminal velocity if they were to jump off.

THE WORLD'S HIGHEST BRIDGE

◀ High and Mighty

http://y2u.be/xIS1ESJ4cOo

"The height of the statue is to remind the youth that the future of the country will be as huge as this," said Indian Prime Minister, Narendra Modi, as he unveiled this 600-foot (182-metre) effigy of independence campaigner Sardar Vallabhbhai Patel. The bronze-clad figure of Patel is twice as high as the Statue of Liberty and dwarfs its nearest rival, the 420-foot (128-metre) High Spring Temple Buddha in China. However, its record is threatened by another Indian construction, the 695-foot (212-metre) memorial to Chhatrapati Shivaji, which is due to be completed in October, 2022.

▲ Ice Crystal Maze

https://youtu.be/eosHKfPAljk

The record for the world's largest snow maze goes to Clint Masse and his family, who built theirs in the small town of Saint Adolphe in Manitoba, Canada. Before it melted, their enormous maze covered an area of 30,022 square feet (2,789 square metres). The walls were 2 feet (60 centimetres) wide and 6 feet (1.8 metres) high, which apparently made it quite cosy inside, but even so you probably wouldn't have wanted to get lost in it for too long as the outside temperature was minus 40 degrees!

Little Big Town

http://y2u.be/O8TsKEtR8VQ

Welcome to Casey, Illinois, just a three-hour drive south of Chicago, USA. It might only have a population of 3,000 but this little town is onto a big thing. In 2011, local man Jim Bolin made a 56-foot (17-metre) wind chime to draw business to his wife's tea shop. He and other town folk then crafted a golf tee (29.5 feet/9 metres), wooden shoes (12 feet/3.6 metres wide), a pitchfork (60 feet/18 metres long), a rocking chair (55 feet/17 metres), a mailbox (33 feet/10 metres), and set of knitting needles (13 feet/4 metres) with crochet hook (6 feet/1.8 metres) – all world-record-sized!

THE MOST-DANGEROUS TUNNEL

◣ Cliffhanger

http://y2u.be/GzJnOrr5RUE

Located in the Taihang Mountains of China, the Guoliang Tunnel is deemed the World's Most Dangerous Tunnel. In 1972, inhabitants of the village of Guoliang dug a tunnel 3,937 feet (1,200 metres) long through the rocky cliff. When opened to traffic it was soon dubbed "the road that does not tolerate any mistakes". A tight squeeze for even one vehicle, it twists and turns past 30 or so "windows", which provide views off the precipice to a tumbling abyss hundreds of feet below.

WILD RECORD BREAKERS

Another scan of the great achievers of the wild world brings forth the slow-motion sloth, the aggressive ant, the super-sized sheep and a rather disgusting beetle.

THE WORLD'S SLOWEST MAMMAL

▼ Turbo Fish

https://youtu.be/VrpNZC-qPn4

What's black, has a sword for an upper jaw and breaks the speed limit underwater? That's no joke – just a description of the black marlin, the fastest fish in the ocean, which can reach speeds of up to 80 mph (129 km/h). They are usually found in the shallow tropical waters of the Indian and Pacific Oceans, close to beaches, islands and coral reefs. Don't worry, though. These slashers are only after small tuna, squid and octopus. The exact number of black marlins in existence isn't known, but it's quite possible they are an endangered species – let's hope it's just that they move too quickly to count.

▲ Sloth Motion

http://y2u.be/OTp8W251aiQ

The three-toed sloth doesn't do anything in a hurry. It likes to sleep for around 10 hours a day, come down from its tree once a week to do its business and occasionally have a (slow) swim. These are the World's Slowest Mammals, averaging a distance of only 0.15 miles (0.24 kilometres) an hour, with a top speed of 6.5 feet (1.98 metres) a minute. They are so slow that algae grow on them. They do, however, have a good excuse; their long claws, ideal for tree life, make walking particularly uncomfortable.

▶ A Dung Deal

http://y2u.be/I1RHmSm36aE

Forget the gorilla or the rhino – the strongest creature on the planet rolls poo into balls and takes it home for supper. The dung beetle is the world's strongest insect and out-muscles every other animal. Dung beetles can pull 1,141 times their own body weight. This is the equivalent of an average person pulling six double-decker buses full of people. Their incredible strength is, of course, useful for pushing those balls of faeces, but also for pushing out rivals trying to enter their under-dung mating tunnels.

THE WORLD'S STRONGEST ANIMAL

◀ Supercow

https://youtu.be/hCk2qocmCuM

It takes something for a cow to go viral, but that's just what happened to Knickers, the Holstein Fresian from Western Australia. When Seven Network's Today Tonight featured the huge steer (a neutered male), this black and white behemoth nearly broke the internet. Measuring well over 6 foot (188 cm) and weighing almost one and a half tonnes, he towers over his cattle pals and is believed to be the biggest steer in the world. It was only Knickers' huge size that saved him from the abattoir, but thankfully his celebrity status has ensured he is looked after, even being chauffeur-driven to country shows in his home state.

SPECTACULAR SCIENCE

Making new discoveries and inventions and exploring deeper and further than ever is the business of the scientist. So it is no surprise that they set some pretty incredible records.

Laser Focus

https://youtu.be/TF0tUbwUcCY

There's no science here. There's no long list of features. This is simply an illuminating demonstration of what the world's strongest handheld laser can do – and it's pretty cool. The laser itself is shiny and sleek, and looks just like a prop from a classic sci-fi movie. It's so powerful it can cause matches to burst into flames, and it can also puncture a football, burn holes in a mobile phone and put on a seriously spectacular light show – electrifying!

▼ Life on Mars

https://youtu.be/Y4gYg2gDNe4

While people across the world were stuck at home in lockdown, Percy had come to the end of a seven-month, 293-million mile (472-million km) journey through space. Perseverance, to give him his full name, was NASA's car-sized rover sent to explore the surface of Mars. In February 2021, it landed in the 28 mile-wide (45 km) Jezero crater north of the planet's equator and sent back the most incredible pictures and, for the first time ever, live sounds of the red planet. The only pity was the absence of little green people. They must have been hiding.

JOURNEY TO THE SURFACE OF MARS

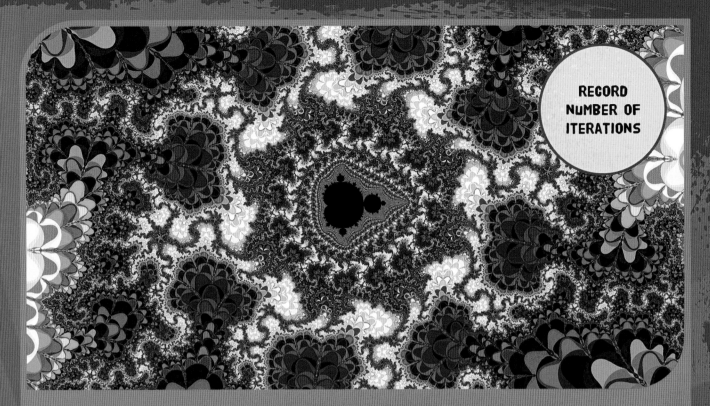

RECORD NUMBER OF ITERATIONS

▲ Do the Math!

http://y2u.be/aSg2Db3jF_4

The Mandelbrot set is a pretty complex mathematical concept that you can look up at your leisure – good luck with that! Mathematicians are still trying to solve some of its mysteries so, if you think you're going to get a simple explanation here, think again! In the meantime, have a look at this because it's awesome. The zooming in on an infinite process creates a mind-blowing set of swirling colourful images, rather like diving into an endless psychedelic pool. This is the record number of iterations, which makes this visual feast well worth including in this book.

▲ In a Galaxy Near You…

https://youtu.be/xC6J4T_hUKg

YouTube channel Hacksmith Industries have form. Making fictional items in comics, movies and video games into real, working prototypes, they have created Captain America's Electromagnet Shield and the Kingsman Umbrella from Fortnite. But no product has been quite so ambitious as their Star Wars Lightsabre. Fuelled by compressed liquid propane gas it produces a beam in a choice of colours, reaches over 2000 degrees Celsius (3600 Fahrenheit) and cuts through metal like a knife through butter. Igniting and retracting at the press of a button, it's real enough to be recognised as the world's first retractable plasma-based lightsabre.

USING THE FORCE

UNLIKELY CELEBRITIES

The millions of YouTube viewers can create the most unlikely celebrity record breakers. Among the surprising super-achievers are a scooting dog and a bunch of dancing hardened criminals.

▼ Exercise Yard

http://y2u.be/vsG1_eee9fg

The Philippines prisoners' dance to "Thriller" was a YouTube hit and is still worth viewing, but this full-body resistance workout by prison inmates in Peru broke their world record for the most people dancing in a prison. The colourful display was the result of three months' practice by around 1,200 prisoners at the overcrowded Lurigancho prison in Lima. The workout saw the prisoners – many of them murderers, drug barons and other serious offenders – strutting their stuff to the sounds and the beats of reggaeton and merengue.

MOST PRISONERS DANCING EVER

▲ To Boldly Go

https://youtu.be/bx_CdBcRexc

"Space is cold and ominous and ugly, and it really threatens death; there's death there. And you look down and there's this warm, nurturing planet." These words could have been spoken by the legendary Captain James T Kirk of the *Starship Enterprise*, but instead they were uttered by William Shatner, the actor who played the captain in the Star Trek TV series and movies. In a bizarre life-imitating-art episode, Shatner, at the age of 90 years, six months and 22 days, boarded Jeff Bezos' Blue Origin on only its second sub-orbital human spaceflight. Breaking the final frontier, he became the oldest person to fly to space.

Cracking Stacking

https://youtu.be/CHudIfQWD50

Here's a record you can practise at home with cheap cardboard cups, but you will have your work cut out beating this young lad. In September 2021, Japan's Rihito Sawada set a new world record for the 3-6-3 cycle stack. The official rules require 12 cups originally placed in two piles of three and one of six. The competitor must then stack each pile into different pyramid arrangements before returning them to their original formation (there are guidelines on speedstacks.com). Under a minute is a good time for a beginner. Rihito does it in 7.540 seconds!

Getting Shirty

https://youtu.be/OtZH8B8gpwA

David Rush is a serial record-breaker. He has set over 150 records in disciplines ranging from chopping balloons with chopsticks to drinking 1.7 pints (1 litre) of lime juice in 17 seconds. Videos of most of these are available on his YouTube channel. This is one anyone can try at home, but you'll need to be pretty nifty to beat David's record of putting on 10 T-shirts in just 15.61 seconds. Go careful, though, because, as you'll see, even a seasoned pro can hurt himself in training.

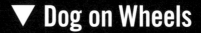

▼ Dog on Wheels

https://youtu.be/8blq71g93B8

He's a three-year-old French sheepdog with a special talent. Ever since he was a puppy, Norman has been climbing on board a scooter and propelling himself along. Norman balances himself on the scooter with his two front paws on the handle and a back paw on the scooter. He uses his other hind paw to push forward. Having already earned the moniker "Norman the Scooter Dog", he then scooted 328 feet (100 metres) in just over 20 seconds – a world record for a dog on a scooter!

BEST CANINE
ON A
SCOOTER

WORLD OF WONDER

Movie star George Clooney famously said, "I go on YouTube when somebody says to look something up." I wonder if he found any of these fabulous clips?

▼ You Know Who

http://y2u.be/EDQqEJWOUH4

In August 2017 a Welsh schoolgirl aged just 13 was named the world's biggest *Doctor Who* super-fan. Lily Connors fell in love with the timelord when she was just three years old. What began as a few second-hand action figures passed on by her father became an astonishing collection of 6,641 items of *Doctor Who* memorabilia. Through pocket-money purchases and gifts from family, friends and even *Doctor Who* actors, her collection includes figurines, sonic screwdrivers, posters and – in pride of place – a Tardis wardrobe made by her father and signed by the 12th Doctor, Peter Capaldi.

▲ Auto Pilot

https://youtu.be/a2tDOYkFCYo

In these worrying climate-threatened times maybe a petrol-fuelled flying car shouldn't be something to get too excited about, but there is undoubtedly something appealingly futuristic about the idea, especially when Klein Vision's AirCar is described as "the lovechild of a Bugatti Veyron and a Cesna 172". On completing a 35-minute flight between international airports at Nitra and Bratislava in Slovakia – the first ever inter-city flying car journey – Slovakian designer Professor Klein enacted the two-and-a-bit minute transformation and, after the wings had folded down along the sides of the car, he proceeded to drive into the city. Pretty cool eh?

LARGEST DR WHO COLLECTION

▼ Thinking Inside the Box

https://youtu.be/v-mnXV_PowM

Unboxing is arguably the most unlikely YouTube phenomenon ever. Millions click on videos just to watch someone else unwrapping something they themselves want. When a video of a small boy unpacking a Spider-Man battery-powered car got over two million views, the Volvo marketing department had an idea: why not make a video of a little lad unboxing a real-life, huge 80-foot (24 metres) long truck? Genius! The resulting video is fun and rather charming, and features the world's largest unboxing – even if it is still a million views behind the Spider-Man car.

WORLD'S LARGEST UNBOXING

Time is Tight

https://youtu.be/k00A_qrzRNs

Big fat watches that weigh your arms down might be just the thing for rappers and bling merchants, but those looking for real style might want to slim it down a bit. Or even a lot. Italian jewellers Bulgari have dominated the "thinnest watch" category for over 50 years, but in 2020, Swiss company Piaget came along with their Altiplano Ultimate Concept. Named after the pancake-flat Altiplano plateau in Bolivia, the watch is just 1/12 inch (2 mm) thick. Don't expect to see one at your local jewellery shop though. They are made to order and will set you back around £250,000.

◀ Out of this World

http://y2u.be/E-mR4LCi9nk

A long time ago, in an era far, far away, a special movie spawned a whole array of related merchandising. In 1977, Steve Sansweet was working at the *Wall Street Journal* and came across a promotional book for an upcoming film called *Star Wars* – it began a lifetime obsession. The film generated a myriad of associated products and Steve began to collect them. Now housed in a 9,000-square-foot (850-square-metre) facility an hour north of San Francisco named Rancho Obi-Wan, his display – the biggest *Star Wars* collection in the world – numbers around 90,000 items with another 200,000 or so in storage awaiting classification.

▼ It's All Relative

http://y2u.be/WebTR66FJPc

Sect leader Ziona Chana has 39 wives – all sharing a 100-room mansion in a holy village in India. The largest family in the world lists 32 sons, 18 daughters, 22 grandsons, 26 granddaughters and seven great-grandchildren all living under one roof. While the youngest wife gets the bedroom next to Ziona, the eldest wife runs the household and organizes the meals, which can see them preparing 30 chickens, peeling 130 pounds (59 kilograms) of potatoes and boiling more than 200 pounds (91 kilograms) of rice.

THE LARGEST FAMILY IN THE WORLD

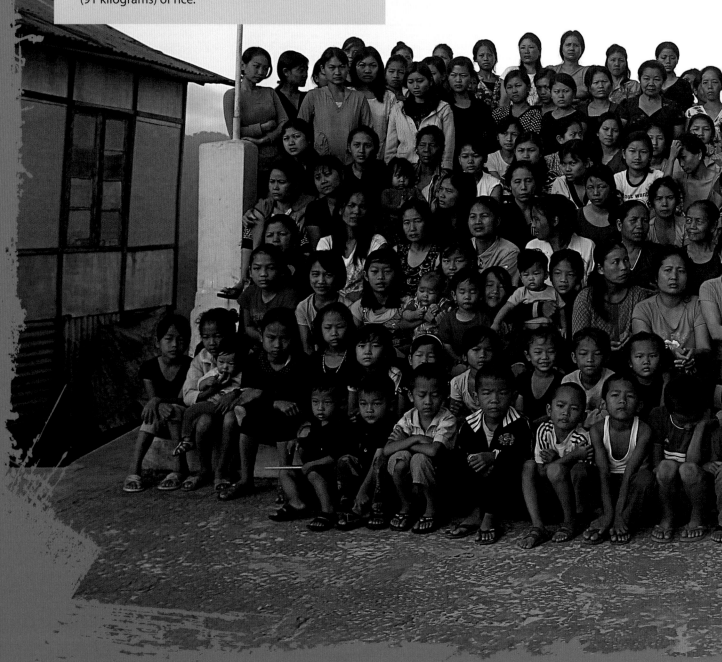

PEOPLE POWER

One day in the far-flung future, everyone will hold a record for something. These guys have already made their mark, but there's a record out there for everyone …

Egged On

https://youtu.be/M6JBEMf7Bu4

The internet can be a funny thing. One minute you're minding your own business walking around with your giant hat full of eggs, the next you've gone viral around the world. That's just what happened to Gregory Da Silva, now known as the "Eggman", from Cape Town, South Africa. A local entertainer, he made himself a 9-foot (3-metre) high hat out of recycled bits and pieces. As if that wasn't enough, he placed 735 eggs in it and still balanced it on his head. All that was left was for Instagram to let the world in on a bizarre but brilliant feat.

▼ Antenna Man

https://youtu.be/NivuCuwZ944

Cyborgs – part-people, part-machines – are the stuff of science fiction films, but Northern Irish artist Neil Harbisson is the first person to be legally recognized as a cyborg: his passport even says he's one. Neil was born completely colour blind and sees the world in shades of black, white and grey. In 2004 he convinced a doctor to implant an antenna into his skull. Called an "eyeborg", it converts colour into vibrations that his brain can interpret. A far cry from scary fictional cyborgs, Neil looks just like a normal person – just a normal person with an antenna.

▶ It's a Twister

http://y2u.be/DwL993LKsFU

Most of us remember going head over heels. Tuck your head in and propel yourself forward. Well, Liu Teng, China's most flexible woman, does something similar – but almost back to front. The 24-year-old, often called the "Queen of Contortion", already held jaw-dropping records for an extreme back-bend off the edge of a table and using her foot to pick up a drinking glass, as well as for the fastest time to travel 65 feet (20 metres) in a contortion roll. In 2017 she broke her own record for the latter in a quite extraordinary and elegant movement.

▶ Heads Up, Bro!

http://y2u.be/At6YhanMLz0

Fans of TV's *Game of Thrones* might recognize the setting for this record as the Great Sept of Baelor. It is, in fact, the Cathedral of Girona in Spain, where Vietnamese circus artists Giang Quoc Co and Giang Quoc Nghiep chose to perform their amazing world-record head-to-head balancing act. The acrobats climbed 90 of the picturesque steps of the cathedral in one minute with one brother balanced on top of the other, using only head-to-head contact. It wasn't the time for the brothers to fall out and, fortunately, they kept clear heads and held any sibling rivalry in check.

WORLD'S BEST BALANCERS

▶ Looking Down the Barrel

https://youtu.be/IJTEo6zY8go

The record for pole-sitting (living in a barrel on top of a pole) was set in 1997 by a 29-year-old South African named Vernon Kruger. He spent 67 days in the barrel, a record that looked unbeatable. That was until January 2020, when it was finally bested – by the now 52-year-old Vernon Kruger! Having taken 23 years to erase the memories of two months spent in a cramped barrel suspended 80 feet (25 metres) above ground, Kruger went back for more. Older and wiser, he extended his record to 78 days. Maybe he'll be back to break it again when he's 75…

▼ Bearded Woman

http://y2u.be/rgQjfcpG7XY

After enduring years of bullying, 25-year-old Harnaam Kaur turned herself into a body-confidence advocate, model and Instagram star. The brave story of the youngest woman to have a full beard is an inspiring one. Diagnosed with polycystic ovaries, Harnaam has had facial hair since the age of 12. She suffered abuse and threats but, at the age of 15, decided to stop hiding and confront gender stereotypes. She never looked back. As she told the *Guardian* newspaper, "They can try to make a freak show out of me, but my voice and my message [are] much stronger than that. I have power in my voice."

RECORD-BREAKING ROBOTS

Science fiction doesn't seem to stay in the films and books for very long these days. Drones are everywhere, maybe keeping a close eye on the dancing robots in the record books.

Beetle Bot

https://youtu.be/OmH0CLXIL-U

Robeetle is less than half an inch, or one centimetre, long and weighs as little as three grains of rice, but it has little legs and antennae that make it look almost alive. Robeetle's real breakthrough, though, is that it runs on methanol, which it carries in its body. This means it can be 10 times smaller than battery-run versions and can run for an hour rather than minutes. The little fellow can crawl along carrying up to 2.6 times its own weight and has no problem with a steep hill. It's the lightest – and probably the cutest – crawling robot ever developed.

▼A Fishy Story

https://youtu.be/kU3yMyuUBA0

Underwater robots are making a big splash in the academic world as scientists look to create the most efficient, strongest and fastest swimming machine possible. In January 2020, a team from the University of Hong Kong set a record for the fastest 50-metre (164-foot) swim by a robotic fish. Its time of 26.79 seconds bettered human female records for both breaststroke (29.40 seconds) and backstroke (26.98 seconds). The four-year project saw the team progress through "White Fish", "Fat Tuna Fish" and "Yellow Tail" prototypes, before settling on "Omega Fish", which they believe can ultimately help in marine exploration, and search and rescue operations.

ONCE I SAW A ROBOT FISH ALIVE

▼ Do the Robot

http://y2u.be/QfocjOJrm3c

Not happy just to take our jobs and drive our cars, robots are now threatening to make boy bands obsolete! Just watch these knee-high Dobi robots go as 1,069 of them set a record for the most robots dancing simultaneously. The nearly perfectly executed dance, which took place in Guangzhou, in China, was managed via a central control system and saw the diminutive automatons get on down in perfect time. Some might find it a little spooky but at least when the robots take over, we can be sure they know how to party!

WORLD'S BEST ROBOTIC DANCERS

Robots, Skips and Jumps

http://y2u.be/HT8BvtfG8w8

ULTIMATE SKIPPING ROBOT PENGUIN

Meet Jumpen, quite possibly the cutest robot ever – although that's not his official world record. Jumpen, a big-eyed, blue-and-white robot penguin, was built at the National Institute of Technology Nara College, in Chiba, Japan. He was the outstanding winner of a skipping competition at a robot convention in Tokyo. For each skip to count, the rope had to complete a 360-degree revolution and be cleared by Jumpen. By the time 60 seconds had elapsed, the diminutive electronic being had completed a world-record 106 skips, successfully clearing the rope every single time. Altogether now, awwww!

SEEING IS BELIEVING

How often do you hear or read of a record and think, "Surely that's just not possible." If only you could see for yourself …

Miniature Machine

http://y2u.be/cSg-yFZ7y0A

In the UK it's called a Heath Robinson contraption, while in the US they call it a Rube Goldberg machine. In France it's an *usine à gaz* (gas refinery), but the Germans come closest to describing it, calling it a *Was-passiert-dann-Maschine* (what-happens-next machine). This video features the smallest ever of these complex devices. Made with incredible precision for an advert for Seiko, this intricate and beautiful machine uses 1,200 mechanical watch parts, some of which are smaller than 1/100 of an inch (1mm) in size. In action, it's mesmerizing and rather magical.

◄ Norwegian Wood

www.youtube.com/watch?v=fXtSlEW1XmE

Alesund in Norway, a town just 280 miles (455 km) from the Arctic Circle, has a long tradition of celebrating mid-summer with an almighty bonfire. In 1904, one out-of-hand fire burned the town to the ground. This did not discourage the townspeople, though, and every year they continue to pile wooden pallets into a massive bonfire which is lit by a brave soul climbing to the top. The tallest of their incredible infernos was this record-breaking bonfire in 2016 which stood 155 feet, 5 inches (47 metres) high and burned for two days.

RECORD-
BREAKING
BONFIRE

▶ There's the Catch

http://y2u.be/7J4xw_g-WsA

Juggling. No! Don't skip this one straightaway. It's short and really impressive. Dutchman Niels Duinker is no children's party juggler; he's a multiple-record-holder and a serial champion in his field. Niels, whose show is entitled "Gravity is a Joke", has been juggling since the age of 12 and claims to have spent over 15,000 hours honing his craft. It seems to be time well spent too. In 2015, he set the bar for the cup-juggling world record at 12 cups. Then, in October 2017, he went two better. Awesome.

WORLD'S BEST CUP JUGGLER

▼ Tunnel Vision

https://www.youtube.com/watch?v=19fQAxys9q8

It's just like something you might see in an action movie, but this is for real! Nobody had ever piloted a plane through a tunnel before, but, on 4 September 2021, Italian race and stunt pilot Dario Costa flew his plane through two concrete car tunnels outside Istanbul. Flying at 152 miles per hour (245 kph), just 3 feet (1 metre) from the ground with just 13 feet (4 metres) between the wing tips and the walls, Costa needed nerves of steel and millisecond reaction times to control the aircraft, especially as he entered the perilous crosswinds between the tunnels.

Blow by Blow

https://youtu.be/gg5KnjdGPOU

The science behind blowing bubbles is simple enough. It's just air wrapped in a thin film of soap. Similarly, a bubble in a bubble is another package of air that just puts a little extra pressure on the outer bubble. Trying to actually blow a bubble inside a bubble is another matter, though, and it's frustratingly difficult – unless you are Taiwanese bubble master Chang Yu-Te. He filled a large bubble with 783 smaller bubbles during an attempt in Taoyuan in January 2021. It's a mesmeric and tense video to watch. No wonder Chang held his heart while he did it.

COOL CAR STUNTS

Car stunts are some of the most exciting clips on the site. These drivers risk life and limb to perform incredible record-breaking tricks and skills on four wheels.

▶ Wheelie Something

http://y2u.be/ggVpCOT9ZqY

Pulling a side-wheelie (driving on just one front and back wheel) in a car is a technically difficult and ludicrously dangerous feat. To drive along on two wheels at breakneck speed is taking it to another level. The speed record on two wheels was last set in 1997, so hats off to Finnish stunt driver Vesa Kivimäki, who finally broke the record in October 2016. Driving a BMW 330 fitted with tyres specially developed by sponsor Nokian, Kivimäki clocked 115.74 mph (186.269 km/h) in his record-breaking jaunt along the runway at Seinajoki Airport in the southwest of Finland.

FASTEST CAR SLALOM...BY A TEEN

▶ Teen Spirit

https://youtu.be/64FjxXJH28Q

When most 16-year-olds are thinking about when they can book their first driving lessons, Chloe Chambers was setting a record for the World's Fastest Slalom. There's no time for mirror, signal, manoeuvre, she's accelerating, swerving and burning rubber from the off in her Porsche 718 Spyder as she slaloms between 51 cones laid out in a straight line 50 feet (15.2 metres) apart, over a distance of 2,500 feet (762 metres). A clean run in just 47.45 seconds means her speed averaged out at over 35mph (58 km/h).

▼ High Roller

https://youtu.be/9yatAJVA_4E

It's a car ad, so naturally this video is slick, shiny and smooth – but that doesn't take anything away from multi-world record-holding stuntman Terry Grant, who attempts a super-impressive feat: the world's longest barrel roll for a production vehicle. Behind the wheel of a Jaguar E-Pace, Terry not only performs a 50-foot (15.3-metre) long jump, he adds in a 270-degree corkscrew-like roll as well. This was the first time a production car had ever completed such an extensive rotation in this kind of stunt.

LONGEST BARREL ROLL FROM A PRODUCTION CAR

Nose Pick

https://youtu.be/RZWI5HasI0Y

Tom Meents is a truck-driving legend. He is a Monster Jam world champion in the racing, freestyle and two-wheel categories. He was the first person to attempt a monster truck backflip and the first to successfully execute a double backflip in a five-ton truck, but this is something different. In August 2020, he pulled a nose wheelie in MAX-D, his 10-foot (3-metre) tall, 12.5-foot (3.5-metre) wide, 10,000-pound (4500-kilo) futuristic SUV monster truck. In an incredible feat of control, the veteran driver quadrupled the existing record with a 209-foot (64-metre) wheelie.

SMASHING THE JUMP RECORD

▼ Ramping It Up

http://y2u.be/L5N7R9Wbe_E

This is the closest you will ever come to seeing a flying car. It was New Year's Eve in Long Beach, California, in 2009, and 20,000 people had come out to see all-action driver Travis Pastrana try something really crazy. Pastrana, a rally champion turned stunt driver, launched his Subaru Impreza STI rally car off a ramp on the Pine Avenue Pier at 91 mph (146.6 km/h). He soared over Rainbow Harbor before successfully landing on a floating barge 269 feet (82 metres) away – almost 100 feet (30 metres) more than the former jump record.

PET RECORDS

These cool creatures have been officially verified as the biggest, sportiest, smallest and most agile.

▶ Monster Bunny

http://y2u.be/SbADYnhHtGg

Darius the rabbit weighs in at 49 pounds (22.2 kilograms) and is the size of a small child. He's the biggest rabbit in the world, but Darius is no freak. His breed, the giant continental, produces large creatures and his mother Alice held the record before him. Five-year-old Darius stretches out to an amazing 4 feet, 4 inches (1.32 metres) long and munches through 4,000 carrots, 120 cabbages and 730 dog bowls of rabbit mix over the year.

THE WORLD'S BIGGEST RABBIT

Who's a Clever Girl Then?

http://y2u.be/unO5whIUF-M

YouTube is full of videos of dogs, and sometimes cats, performing stunts – but Kili the Senegal parrot can match them trick for trick. She claims an unofficial world record by pulling off 20 tricks in just under two minutes. Her feats begin with the customary parrot skills such as rope climbing and nodding. Nothing remarkable there, but carry on watching and you'll see Kili go bowling, match rings to pegs and perform a basketball slam dunk. Worthy of the record books, surely?

◢ Ballpark Figure

https://youtu.be/1QTnTc7wVhs

Just watch Macho go! In September 2021, the Jack Russell terrier skirted around the bases at the Dodger Stadium in Los Angeles, completing his home run in only 21.06 seconds. At all the bases he even popped balloons, put there by his owner to make sure he touched each one. Macho was single-minded in his quest to set the record for fastest dog around a Major League Baseball diamond, running at a speed of around 12 miles per hour (20 kph), and he avoided any temptation to stop for a sniff or to cock his leg. As a reward, he received a well-deserved rib supper.

FASTEST CANINE HOME RUN

Dynamic Duo

https://youtu.be/tQDkYJ-jxgM

Lollipop and Sashimi haven't exactly taken the world of extreme sports by storm, but the duo make up for it in cuteness. Lollipop is a deaf five-year-old Boston terrier, while Sashimi is a seven-year-old tabby cat, and together they have formed a record-breaking partnership. According to their dog trainer owner, the pair came up with the feat themselves, when Sashimi jumped on Lollipop's scooter (of course!). Instead of turfing her off like any normal dog, Lollipop began pushing his pussy passenger. Soon they were covering 16.4 feet (5 metres) in just 4.37 seconds – a record time for a dog and cat on a scooter!

▶ My Little Pony

http://y2u.be/6XQtd9cTGFM

Here's another Einstein. Smaller than most human babies he was just 14 inches (35.5 centimetres) high at birth, weighing only 6 pounds (2.7 kilograms). Now fully grown, Einstein stands 20 inches (50.8 centimetres) high and is officially the World's Smallest Stallion. The smallest horse, Thumbalina, is slightly shorter but, unlike her, Einstein is not a dwarf, he is just a mini miniature horse. He does, however, have a big personality. He has his own Facebook page, has appeared on *Oprah* and even had a book written about him.

THE WORLD'S SMALLEST STALLION

APP APTITUDE

It's the digital age and a new breed of record-breakers – tweeters, texters, vloggers and bloggers – is on the rise. These guys are setting amazing new standards – a bit more impressive than managing to remember your eight-digit password.

Avatar Assembly

http://y2u.be/HPUjg-6nufw

Fans of *World of Warcraft* – the most popular multi-player online role-playing game in the world – were briefly distracted from pursuing quests and fighting monsters to witness a record-breaking diorama. To promote a new expansion of their game at a convention, producers Blizzard created a 1,300-square-foot (400-square-metre) 3D battle, complete with over 10,000 3D printed figures. And just to make the world's largest video-game diorama completely fabulous, every character on the battlefield corresponded to convention attendees' avatars, including their armour, race and weaponry. Great! Now back to the game…

◄ Reality Check

http://y2u.be/yLGMEt3RkAg

There are worse places to spend 36 hours – the dentist, a motorway service station or your aunt's wedding, perhaps? Jack McNee from Sydney, Australia, did his record time in the virtual world. There are many pastimes available on VR, including colonizing alien planets or exploring the ocean, but Jack played *Tilt Brush* for the whole time! With the device strapped to his face for a day and a half, he painted and played *Hangman* and *Pictionary* with his YouTube live-stream viewers. As for eating and comfort breaks, Jack relied on his trusty staff to guide him.

LONGEST TIME SPENT IN VIRTUAL REALITY

▼ Fastest Finger

http://y2u.be/zXjTPnV8ZvM

Fancy a go at being the fastest texter in the world? Here's your chance. Get your phone or iPad set up and see how fast you can type (or swype) the following sentence: "The razor-toothed piranhas of the genera Serrasalmus and Pygocentrus are the most ferocious freshwater fish in the world. In reality they seldom attack a human." Did you make it under 17.5 seconds? If you did, get your claim off to the record-keepers. If not, watch this clip of record-holder Abdul Basit showing just how it's done.

THE FASTEST TEXTER OF ALL TIME

Perfectly in Sync

https://youtu.be/r0y59TyB2_w

Who said Tik Tok was just for the under-18s? The most-liked post on the site belongs to a 24-year-old US Navy veteran who moved to Texas from her native Philippines when she was 13. Bella Poarch only took to the app after leaving the Navy in 2020, but mastered the media almost immediately. Within just four months, the 10-second video of her lip-syncing to 'Sophie Aspin Send' by Millie B had gone viral. Her simple, close-up, expressive, zoomed-in video had garnered over 50 million likes and, just like that, a star was born.

SPORTS HEROES

From the sublime skills of Cristiano Ronaldo to the stars of quirky sports such as bog snorkelling or walking on your hands, these people are all record heroes.

RECORD INTERNATIONAL GOAL-SCORER

Flaming Flips

https://youtu.be/13colLcrBag

Yeah, fire-breathing… yawn. Hang on, though, this is fire-breathing with a twist – quite literally. In November 2017, on the set of Aussie morning talk show *Studio 10*, extreme acrobat Aiden Malacaria attempted the record for the most fire-breathing, full-twist backflips in one minute. Each jump had to be a complete 360-degree backwards flip and, whilst airborne, Aiden needed to perform a 360-degree lateral spin, and blow a flame, without falling. Incredibly he manages ten flame-accompanied flips, two more than the existing record. Someone really should make it a little more difficult!

▲ Goal Focused

https://youtu.be/aS1E_ejn7Po

"Records are meant to be broken. I'm happy such a great player will surpass me, because I consider Ronaldo among the top three players ever." So said Ali Daei, the Iranian footballer who, since 2003, had scored more international goals than any other player. His record stood at 109 goals, which many thought would never be beaten, but Portugal's Cristiano Ronaldo had other ideas. As his career stretches on and on, he consistently continues to find the back of the net. He equalled the record in the 2020 Euros, scored twice against the Republic of Ireland in September 2021, and has since taken his national-team total to 115.

Seconds Out

http://y2u.be/BSp60Y-eLR0

Zolani Tete versus Siboniso Gonya wasn't top of the bill at Belfast in November 2017. The next morning, however, it was the bout people were talking about, even though it lasted just 11 seconds and consisted of a single punch. WBO bantamweight champion Tete was expected to win – just not like this. The 29-year-old South African laid out his countryman, landing a brutal right hook six seconds after the opening bell. The referee officially ended the contest five seconds later as the challenger lay sprawled out. It was the quickest-ever world-title fight in the history of boxing.

▼ Muddy the Waters

http://y2u.be/UoRXZOQBsSQ

The World Bog Snorkelling Championship, first held in 1985, takes place every August at the dense Waen Rhydd peat bog, near Llanwrtyd Wells in Mid-Wales. Bog snorkelling requires competitors to complete two consecutive 60-yard (55-metre) lengths of a water-filled trench cut through a peat bog. Competitors must wear snorkels and flippers, and complete the course without using conventional swimming strokes, relying on flipper power alone. Andrew Holmes is the record holder with a time of 84 seconds.

Head's Up

https://youtu.be/4Isf7TNQF_Q

Falling headfirst down the stairs is an unfortunate occurrence for many people, but Li Longlong, an acrobat from mainland China, takes the opposite route. He goes upstairs on his head. With incredible powers of balance, stamina, upper body strength and a fair dollop of derring-do, Li takes on a vertical staircase. The rules state that only his head is allowed to touch each step and there's little time for recovery as he can only rest for five seconds between stairs. After an amazing 36 steps, he collects his record-breaking certificate – and possibly a bottle of headache pills!

THE WORLD BOG SNORKELLING CHAMPION

▲ Danger Ball

https://youtu.be/1JUn8MsEyPs

If playground tag seems a little rough to you then you are probably wise to steer clear of Buzkashi, the most dangerous game in the world. Widely played in central Asia, especially in Afghanistan, where it is the national sport, the game is centuries old. Although rules vary from area to area, it is played by two teams of 10 to 12 players on horseback and lasts between 90 minutes and three hours. The object is to carry a goat carcass to a marked circle. That's basically it. Pulling the carcass from another player is allowed and hitting other horses and players is all part of the action.

MOST DANGEROUS TEAM SPORT

COOL SPORTS RECORDS

From frantic four-legged running to bionic shoes, the quest for sporting perfection never ends and with it comes the sound of clattering records.

No Business like Toe Business

https://youtu.be/wtI5Ry0YB2c

Toe wrestling was invented in 1974 by customers of the Royal Oak Pub in Wetton, Derbyshire, in an attempt to find a sport at which Britain could be the world's best. It was shelved two years later when a Canadian visitor was proclaimed champion. In 1994, the pub's landlord found the rules and re-instigated the game, which looks like an aggressive form of footsie and is similar to arm-wrestling but with toes. Since then, a British man has dominated the sport: Alan "Nasty" Nash, who is looking to win his seventeenth championship.

FOUR-LEGGED-SPRINT RECORD HOLDER

▶ Four Legs Good

http://y2u.be/A3rcWarJOe0

Kenici Ito, a 29-year-old man from Tokyo, Japan, spent over eight years perfecting a four-legged running style based on the wiry Patas monkey of Africa. Neighbours would see him walking around on all fours and he was even shot at by mistake by hunters when training in the mountains. It all paid off in 2012, when Ito incredibly ran 100 metres in less than 20 seconds. He now runs in four-legged races but admits he is still beaten by a fast dog.

Captain Marvel

https://youtu.be/VI312DX1Zrk

During the Covid-19 pandemic in 2020, a 99-year-old former serviceman captured the hearts of the nation. Captain Tom Moore set out to raise £1,000 for the National Health Service by walking 100 laps of his garden before his 100th birthday. Within 25 days he had raised £38.9 million, including contributions from over 160 countries. In doing this he smashed the record for the most money raised by an individual charity walk. He soon added another record when "You'll Never Walk Alone", his duet with Michael Ball, made him the oldest person to reach number one in the UK charts. In a sad postscript to the story, Captain Tom died after contracting the virus early in 2021.

By a Nose

https://youtu.be/LuCpE5CoFtU

Brad Byers is a one-man record book. He's been breaking records for over 20 years with all kinds of scary feats, including the most swords swallowed and twisted, lying on a bed of nails while his brother drives over him on a quad bike and inserting a speeding drill up his nose. Here's one of his records you can try at home. It looks easy at the hands – or nose – of a master, but don't worry, it's pretty safe – as long as you return the cash to the owner!

▲ World at his Feet

https://youtu.be/Uuj3cDaOqzo

Chinonso Eche. Remember the name, because in a handful of years he could be lighting up the Premier League, La Liga or the Bundesliga. Right now, he is just a 12-year-old boy from Nigeria with prodigious freestyling footballing skills and ambitions to be world famous. In 2021, "Amazing Kid Eche", as he has been nicknamed, took the first steps to realising his ambition when he broke the record for the most consecutive soccer touches in one minute while balancing a ball on the head. It's a masterclass in control and balance – and thank heavens there wasn't a defender trying to hack him down at the time.

WHAT A RECORD!

If God had meant us to fly, he'd have given us wings ... then again, he did give us skateboards, huge swings, dodgy planes and long bungee elastic!

The Only Way is Down

http://y2u.be/JXyQ3N4S5oc

Marc Sluszny is the most extreme adventurer in the world. He's set a world record in bungee jumping, dived with a great white shark and represented Belgium in tennis, fencing, yachting and bobsleigh. In 2012, Marc found a new hobby – running down a building. Here he is completing a vertical run down the side of the Belgacom tower in Brussels. The tower is 335 feet (102 metres) high and he sprinted down the outside of it in a time of 15.5 seconds – a new world record.

▼ Zip trip

https://youtu.be/81ebJIJZ8oI

Velocity 2, the fastest zipline in the world, is sited near Bangor in North Wales. It's really just like the zip ride at your local park – you clip yourself onto the wire and push yourself off the platform and into the air. Except this ride is located on the top of a quarry often shrouded in mist, riders fly over 500 feet (152 metres) above the water, go from 0 to 60 mph (96 km/h) in under 10 seconds and reach a top speed of 125 mph (201 km/h) – and your mum isn't even there to catch you at the bottom!

▶ Boarded Up

https://youtu.be/iVMyG6AO-XQ

For years, "the 1080" (in which a skateboarder makes three full revolutions while in the air) has been one of the holy grails of skateboarding. American Tom Schaar completed a 1080-degree turn in 2012, but on a mega ramp that gave him a big advantage. In May 2020 "the 900" record set by legend Tony Hawk in 1999 was finally beaten – by an 11-year-old Brazilian called Gui Khury. Gui's father put the success down to the Covid-19 pandemic, which had given his son the time to perfect the stunt. It's good to know that someone used the time productively!

THE WORLD'S FIRST "1080"

▲ Big Rush

http://y2u.be/FrY6OJk-z0I

The Moses Mabhida Stadium in Durban, South Africa, was built for the FIFA World Cup in 2010. The imposing 54,000-seater venue, instantly recognizable from its beautiful white arches, now hosts sports matches, events and the world's only stadium swing – the biggest swing of any kind. Those venturing to the top of the stadium are afforded a fabulous 360-degree view of Durban and a chance to ride the Big Rush Adrenaline Swing. This thrilling experience begins with a 288-foot (88-metre) freefall followed by a massive 721-foot (220-metre) arc that takes the rider into the centre of the stadium. Not for the faint-hearted!

WORLD'S BIGGEST SWING

▲ Flight of Fancy

http://y2u.be/KUlZQ3JyrBM

Man cracked the secret of flying more than a hundred years ago, but you wouldn't think it watching the Red Bull Flugtag. Held annually since 1992 all around the world, the "flying day" event sees participants build and then pilot their homemade flying machines off a 28-foot (8.5-metre) high flight deck. Judged for distance, creativity and showmanship, the aerodynamic qualities of the aircraft are often questionable. Many teams crash pretty instantly and chaotically into the waters below. However, in 2013 the Chicken Whisperers team set a distance record of 258 feet (78.64 metres) in Long Beach, California.

Hover bother

https://youtu.be/ET7Yva3C01w

The 1989 movie *Back to the Future II* saw Marty McFly use a hoverboard to escape from Griff Tannen and his gang when he visits 2015. This stunt was a few years late, but in July 2021, Kyxz Mendiola, an inventor from the Philippines, all padded up, all in black and looking like he had stepped out of a sci-fi movie, took to the air. He stood upright on his electric hoverboard for almost two miles (2894 metres) in a record-breaking, seven-and-a-half minute flight in which he floated 30 feet (10 metres) high over the boats of Subic Bay, on the west coast of the Philippines island of Luzon.

LONGEST RED BULL FLUGTAG FLIGHT

153

HAIR-RAISING RECORDS

There are some special people for whom "doing their hair" doesn't mean a few minutes with a brush and a mirror. Hairstyles, beards, moustaches and other follicular follies are their step to stardom ...

▶ Good Hair Day

https://youtu.be/EF8fYy6Jr0s

It had its heyday in the 1970s, but the big afro is well and truly back, with popstars such as Rhianna and Beyoncé, and sportsmen like Leroy Sané and Colin Kaepernick, helping to bring the bold hairstyle back into vogue. But none have gone as big as American fashion designer Simone Williams. She has been growing and styling her hair naturally for over nine years, and in December 2020 discovered that her 'fro had reached 8.07 inches (20.5 centimetres) tall and 8.85 inches (21.6 centimetres) wide, breaking a world record that had lasted since 2012.

WORLD'S LARGEST AFRO

◀ Teen Queen

https://youtu.be/aMPomLI5JMU

After a bad haircut at the age of six, Nilanshi Patel from Gujarat, India, swore she would never have her locks cut again. She was true to her word – 10 years later she had the longest hair on a teenager in the world. That was in 2018. Two years after that she still held the title and her tresses were now 6 feet 3 inches (190 centimetres) long – a full 8 inches (20.3 centimetres) more than her own height!

▼ Hard to Handlebar

http://y2u.be/PKzBzDY5I50

Ram Singh Chauhan of India is the proud owner of the world's longest moustache, stretching an incredible 14 feet (4.27 metres). Now 57, he started growing his moustache in 1970. It isn't an easy life – Chauhan spends an hour every day cleaning and combing his moustache, and when it is not on proud display, he has to neatly wrap it around his neck. However, it has brought him prestige and some fame, with appearances in Bollywood films as well as the 1983 James Bond film *Octopussy*.

▲ Hair-raising Story

https://youtu.be/R8vAxZq4N7Q

It's been a long journey for Joe Grisamore. In 2006, he began to grow his hair in an attempt to break the tallest Mohawk spike record. By 2013, his spike had grown to around 6 feet (1.8 metres) high but, after swimming during his honeymoon in the Caribbean, his hair was so damaged by saltwater that he had to shave it off. Undaunted, he began again, this time aiming for the full Mohican record. By 2020, his hair was long enough for a stylist, armed with just a can of hairspray, to mould it into a magnificent 42-inch (106.7-centimetre) creation, which smashed the existing record.

SETTING YOUR OWN RECORD

Even in our wildest dreams, we can't hope to emulate the feats of some of the record breakers in this book. The achievements of Usain Bolt or Cristiano Ronaldo are the result of a talent and dedication possessed by few. Others are born to be record breakers by dint of an exceptional physical attribute – a long tongue, big feet – whether they like it or not! Still, the budding record breaker need not despair. There are plenty of videos in this book to inspire anyone to write their name in the history books.

Perhaps you already have a unique skill or hobby that can rival the record holders. For example, you might have a great talent for skipping or licking your nose or you might have quick reflexes or a steady hand. It is likely that your particular skill isn't yet at the level of the current record holders; most of the achievements in the book are due to practice and hard graft. Start working at it now, though, and who knows what heights you will reach?

You don't have to possess a great physical skill to enter the record books. There are plenty of other entries that are equally impressive. Mental agility is a popular area and there are incredible feats of reading, mathematics and memory; world-beating collections – of anything from TV-show memorabilia to cereal packets – form a fascinating aspect of record breaking; and someone needs to organize the large-scale gatherings that beat records.

If you need to research your goal, go online and check the existing record. Some in this book did just that and discovered it was a target they could aspire to and eventually beat. There are various organizations, including sporting bodies, who keep their own statistics. Most famously, the *Guinness Book of Records* (www.guinnessworldrecords.com) has been keeping records since 1955 and has a comprehensive database and an online application process.

If you are looking to set a more unusual record, it might be worth consulting recordsetter.com, where you will find inspiration and challenges for all kinds of records – many of which can be attempted in your own kitchen or bedroom. If you don't fancy taking on other people's records, you can always invent your own category. You'll definitely have a record, but don't count on keeping it for long – it's a mighty competitive record-breaking world.

INDEX

PICTURE CREDITS